IS THIS GUY FOR REAL?

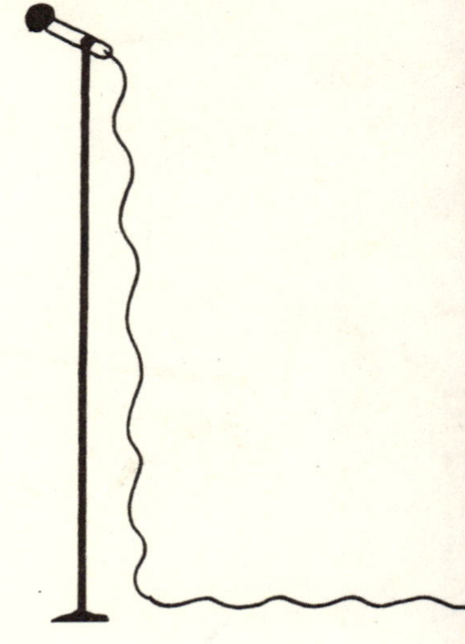

IS THIS GUY FOR REAL?

THE UNBELIEVABLE ANDY KAUFMAN

BOX BROWN

First Second
NEW YORK

THIS IS ANDY KAUFMAN.
HE IS A YOUNG BOY GROWING UP
IN LONG ISLAND, NEW YORK.

HE'S WATCHING TV.

HERE I COME TO SAVE THE DAY!

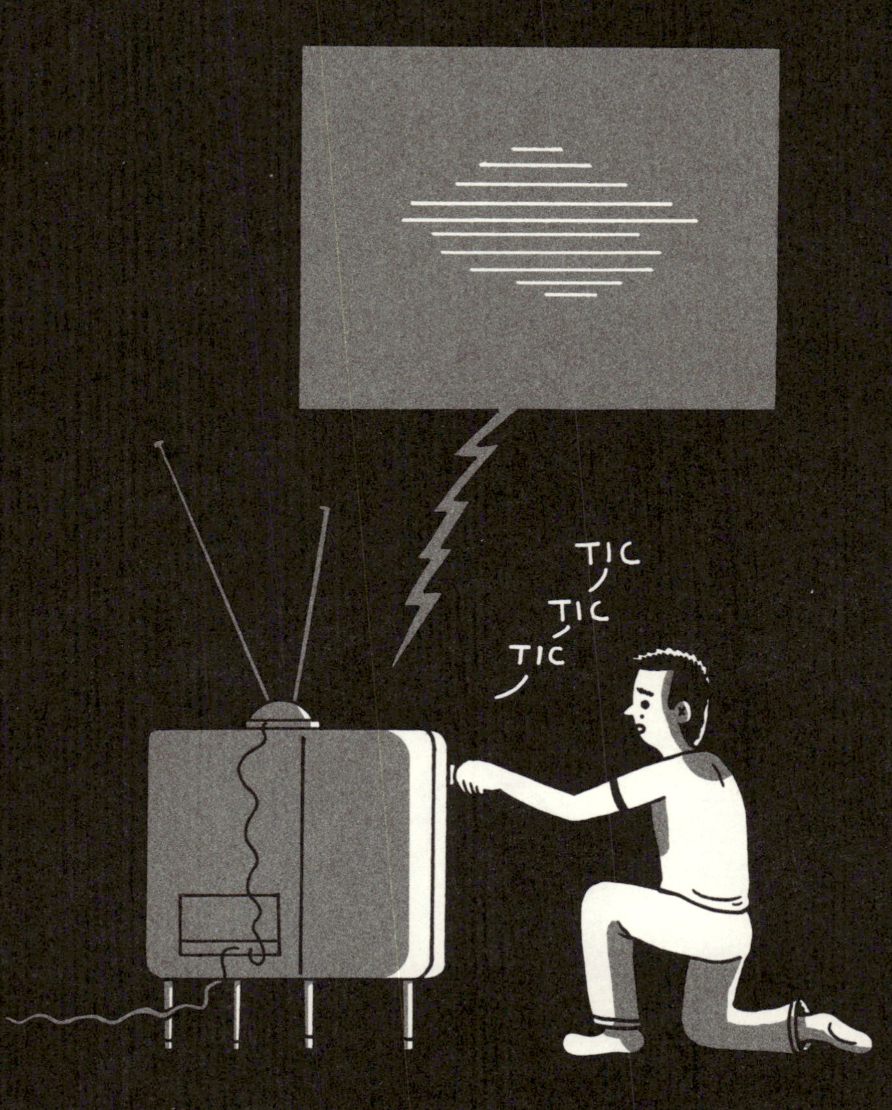
TIC
TIC
TIC

HEY, GUYS... LET'S ROCK!!

"ELVIS PRESLEY, "BLUE HAWAII," 1961
ROCK-A-HULA, BABY.
ROCK-A-HULA...

-A-HULA ROCK-A-HULA GOTTA HULA LU

ROCK-A-HULA

TIC
TIC
TIC
TIC

"NATURE BOY" BUDDY ROGERS

BOO!!
BOOOO!!

THAT'S RIGHT!

"NATURE BOY" BUDDY ROGERS, ONE OF THE MOST COLORFUL WRESTLERS IN THE WORLD TODAY...

NOT ONE OF... THE!
THE!
THE!

THE GREATEST WRESTLING ANYONE'S EVER SEEN HAS COME OUT OF THIS BODY.

TO A NICER GUY...
BOO
BOO

...THIS COULDN'T HAVE HAPPENED.
BOO

HA!!
BOO

STRUT

STRUT

BUDDY ROGERS'S COSTUMING WAS LIKE NOTHING ELSE OUT THERE.

HE LOOKED SO PRETTY.

NO ONE HAD EVER SEEN ANYTHING LIKE HIM ON TELEVISION.

AND THEY HATED HIM.

THE WRESTLING FANS HATED BUDDY ROGERS.

BOOO

ABSOLUTELY ABHORRED HIM.

BOOOOO

THE GREATEST WRESTLING ANYONE'S EVER SEEN HAS COME OUT OF THIS BODY!!
HA!

ANDY'S BROTHER
YOU HEAR ME, MICHAEL!

I AM...
...THE GREATEST WRESTLER EVER!!

NATURE BOY!
BUDDY ROGERS!

HAH HA!!
STRUT

COME ON, LET'S WRESTLE LIKE THEY DO ON TV! I'LL BE BUDDY ROGERS!

OK... BUT I WANNA BE A GOOD GUY.
MAYBE JOHNNY VALENTINE.

FIRST YOU PUT ME IN A HEADLOCK, THEN DO THAT ONE MOVE. THEN I'LL GRAPEVINE YOUR LEGS.

YOU'RE DONE FOR, ROGERS!
NEVER! NEVER, VALENTINE!!
I'M THE GREATEST!

OW!! AHH!!
MY NECK!!

ARE YOU
FAKIN' IT?
NO!!

I'LL GO GET
DAD...
...SORRY.

LOOKS LIKE YOU'RE GONNA HAVE TO BE IN TRACTION FOR A FEW WEEKS, ANDY.

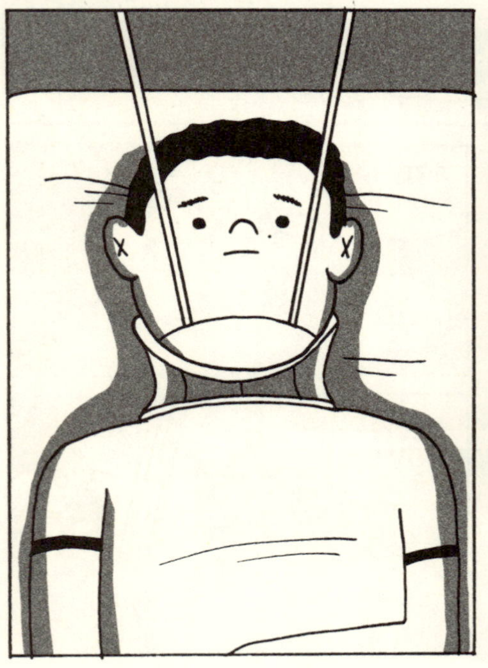

JUST LIKE BUDDY ROGERS.

ANDY RECOVERED FROM HIS INJURIES.
ELVIS IN VIVA LAS VEGAS
ELVIS VIVA L VEGAS

BUT HE COULDN'T STOP IMITATING HIS HEROES.

(HUMMING ELVIS)

AND ELVIS PRESLEY WAS AT THE TOP OF THE LIST.

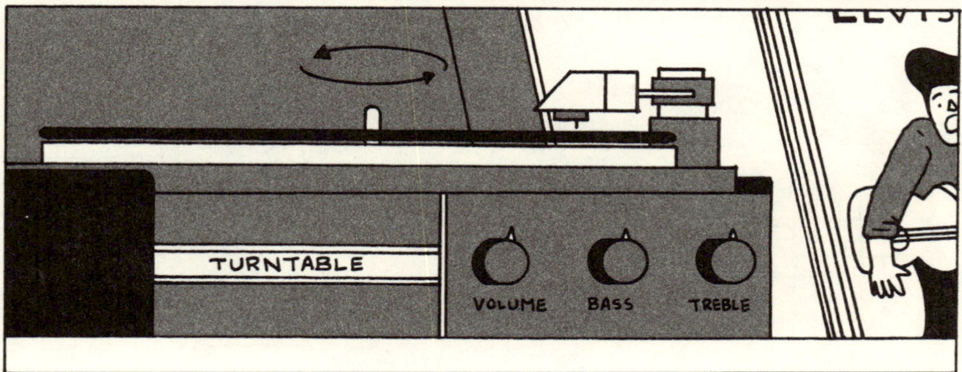
TURNTABLE
VOLUME
BASS
TREBLE

ANDY'S GRANDPARENTS WERE HIS BIGGEST FANS.

GRANDMA PEARL WATCHED WRESTLING WITH ANDY.

COMMACK ARENA 9-28
8 O'CLOCK BELL TIME

GASP!

COMMACK... LONG ISLAND!!

DAD!! WRESTLING IS COMING TO LONG ISLAND! COME ON! IT'LL BE FUN FOR EVERYONE! THE WHOLE FAMILY!!

NO.

NO WAY.

I SAID NO.

MAYBE...

WHEN IS IT?

AFTER WORK? NO WAY, TRAFFIC.

AWW...

OKAY. FINE.
SHRUG

HEY, DAD! THIS TRAFFIC ISN'T SO BAD!!

HONK

WE MADE IT! COME ON MICHAEL!!
DING!
DING!
LONG ISLAND ARENA

THE HEROES:
"COWBOY" BOB ELLIS AND
JOHNNY VALENTINE

VS.

THE VILLAINS:
THE
FABULOUS KANGAROOS

BOO BOOO

TWO FALLS TO A FINISH.
ELLIS AND VALENTINE WON THE FIRST FALL HANDILY.

THEN "COWBOY" BOB ELLIS SUFFERED AN INJURY!
THE KANGAROOS TOOK THE SECOND FALL.

THEN COWBOY BOB RETURNED!
THE GOOD GUYS WIN!!

WHAT A NIGHT! HUH, DAD?
TRY TO GO TO SLEEP. YOU BOTH HAVE SCHOOL TOMORROW!!

* BRUNO SAMMARTINO; WORLD CHAMPION 1963–1971 & 1973–1977

DING-DING

THEY CAN GET AWAY WITH ANYTHING!

QUIET BACK THERE!!

HEY, KIDS!!
LET'S WATCH SOME CARTOONS!!
GRANDPA PAUL HAMMED IT UP AT THE KIDS' PARTIES.
HAW!! 
HAHA!
HAW-HAW!
HAHAHA!!
HAHHHA!!

ANDY WATCHED GRANDPA PAUL JOKE AND DO OLD MAGIC TRICKS.

AND ANDY THOUGHT:
I CAN DO THIS.

HE GOT RIGHT TO PERFECTING HIS ACT...

SUDDENLY ANDY'S DAD WAS CHAUFFEURING HIM TO KIDS' PARTIES ALL OVER LONG ISLAND.

EXIT 62
97
STONY BROOK
½ MILE

TWEEN ANDY KAUFMAN WAS THE PARTY ENTERTAINMENT FOR LITTLE KIDS. PAID GIGS!

TIME FOR CARTOONS!

HOORAY!!

ANOTHER SCHOOL ASSEMBLY. USUALLY ANDY WOULD'VE BEEN SCREWING AROUND, BUT TODAY HE WAS ENTRANCED.
BABATUNDE OLATUNJI!
BOBBA-BOBBA-BOBBA-BOBBA

BOBBA-BOBBA-BOBBA-BOBBA

ANDY'S MIND WAS BLOWN.
BOBBA
BOMBA
BOOMB
BA

CHANGED FOREVER.
BOO
BAD
BOMBA

KABOOBOOBKABOOK

I COULD DO THIS...
BAK
BA

BET I'LL DO THE MOST CHIN-UPS.
SHUT UP, KAUFMAN!
ANDY, YOU GET UP THERE! NO SCREWING AROUND.

GOT IT, COACH.

NO FUNNY STUFF.
CHIN-UPS ONLY.

34!

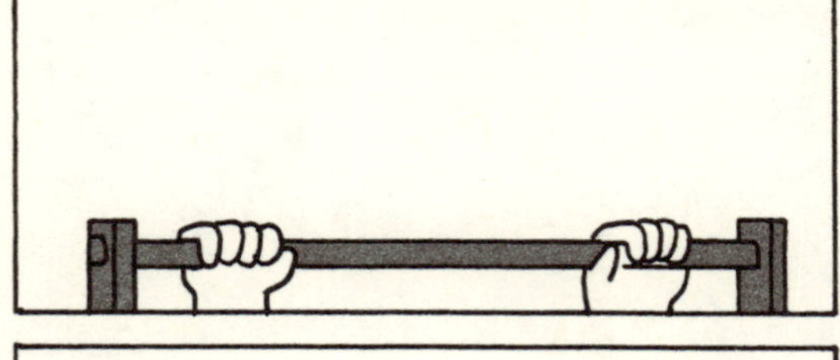

35!
HOUGHA!

THE MOST CHIN-UPS IN THE CLASS: ANDY KAUFMAN WITH THIRTY-FIVE!
YEAH!

KAUFMAN, IF YOU COULD DO SO MANY CHIN-UPS, HOW COME YOU'RE SUCH A TURD??

HAHA... UH...
I DON'T KNOW.

HUFF-PUFF HUFF-PUFF

LISTEN, GENTLEMEN, THIS IS WRESTLING. NOT THAT CRAP THEY SHOW ON SATURDAY MORNING WITH THE CARTOONS.

PFFT... LOOK AT KAUFMAN.

TWEEEEEEEEEET!!

HOOH
WA!!

DANG!!
KAUFMAN IS NUTS!

CRUNCH
WRESTLING COMING TO NEW YORK CITY!!
CORN BITS

!
MADISON SQUARE GARDEN!

BRUNO SAMMARTINO

VS.
BUDDY ROGERS CHAMPION

WRESTLING - NO TV

MAD. SQ. GARDEN | FRI. MAY 17

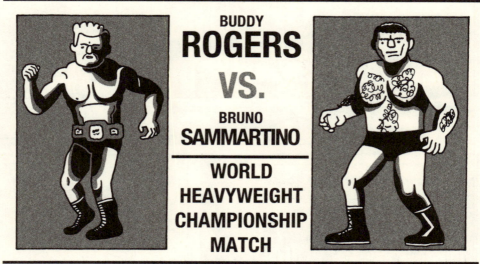

BUDDY
ROGERS
VS.
BRUNO
SAMMARTINO

WORLD HEAVYWEIGHT CHAMPIONSHIP MATCH

GREAT SCOTT VS. GREAT MORTIMER

PEDRO MORALES VS. WILLIE BATH

UNITED STATES TAG TEAM TITLE MATCH

BRUTE BERNARD &
SKULL MURPHY
VS.
BOBO BRAZIL &
DORY DIXON

LAST DAY OF SCHOOL AND WRESTLING!!
THIS IS THE GREATEST DAY OF MY LIFE.

BRUNO'S GONNA WHIP ROGERS.

HA! HA!

NO ONE CAN BEAT ROGERS, MAN.

HE'LL CHEAT TO WIN, THAT'S WHY!
HEH!

ROGERS WILL BE WALKING OUT WITH THE BELT TONIGHT. I'LL BET ANYTHING.

BUDDY ROGERS ONCE BEAT A GUY SO BAD...

...THAT THEY TOOK THE GUY OUT ON A STRETCHER.

OH, YOU'RE HURT OVER THERE, HUH??
UGGGHHH!!

THEN BUDDY KICKED OVER THE STRETCHER!
AND THE GUY FELL OFF!

I AM THE GREATEST!!
MADISON SQUARE GARDEN
MAY 17, 1963

STRUT
STRUT

STRUT

STRUT
STRUT

STRUT
STRUT

HEY, KID, SIT DOWN! IT'S STARTING!!

EVERYTHING WAS GOING GREAT!

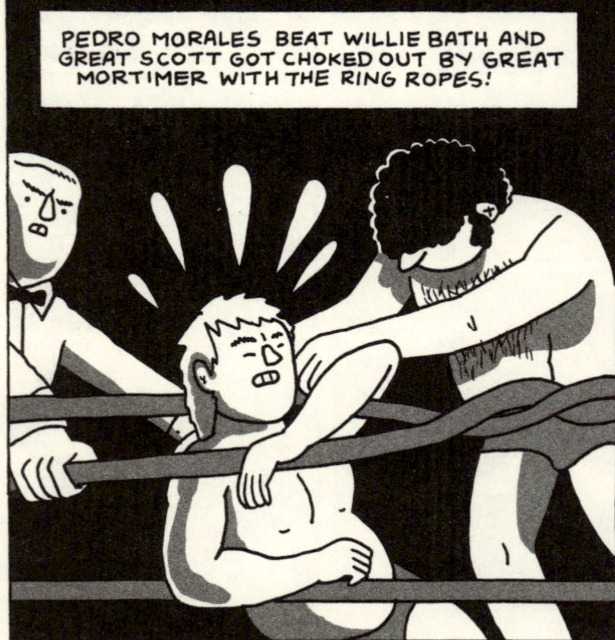

FINALLY, IT WAS THE MAIN EVENT.
HAND IT OVER, ROGERS!

DING!
DING!

SUDDENLY, SAMMARTINO FLIPPED ROGERS UP OVER HIS SHOULDER AND PUT HIM IN A "BACKBREAKER."

MADISON SQUARE GARDEN WAS SHOCKED!

ONCE THE TRUTH SETTLED IN, THE PEOPLE REALIZED THEIR HERO HAD WON THE TITLE IN FORTY SECONDS!

EVERYONE EXPLODED!

HOO-RAY!!

BRUNO!!

AFTER THAT ANDY STOPPED WATCHING WRESTLING FOR A DECADE.

EVERYONE WAS RIGHT ABOUT WRESTLING. IT WAS FIXED. BUDDY ROGERS WOULD NOT QUIT IN FORTY SECONDS!!

THE MAGIC WAS JUST GONE.

IN REALITY, BUDDY ROGERS HAD STOPPED SELLING OUT BUILDINGS.

IT WAS TIME FOR HIM TO GET OUT OF THE WAY.

WRESTLING JUST ISN'T THE SAME AS IT USED TO BE.

ELVIS PRES
ELVIS
ELVIS
ELVIS IS BACK!
ANDY REMAINED AN OBSESSIVE ELVIS FAN INTO HIS TEENS.
ELVIS
ELVIS G.I. BLUES
PRESLEY
ELVIS
ELVIS
ELVIS DO THE CLAM
ELVIS PRESLEY
EVEN AS EVERYONE DRIFTED INTO BEATLEMANIA.
ELVIS
ELVIS
ELVIS PRESLEY
"THANK YOU VERY MUCH..."

IT'S ON, IT'S ON!

THERE HE IS!!

ANDY WAS THE ONLY KID IN HIS HIGH SCHOOL WHO CARED ABOUT ELVIS'S "'68 COMEBACK SPECIAL."
ANDY! COME ON! WE CAN'T SEE!!

EVEN WHEN ANDY BECAME A PUNK TEENAGER...

...HE'D GET DRUNK AND PUT ON ELVIS RECORDS.

COME ON, ANDY!
NOT AGAIN.
PUT ON THE STONES, MAN.

VIVA LAS VEGAS!

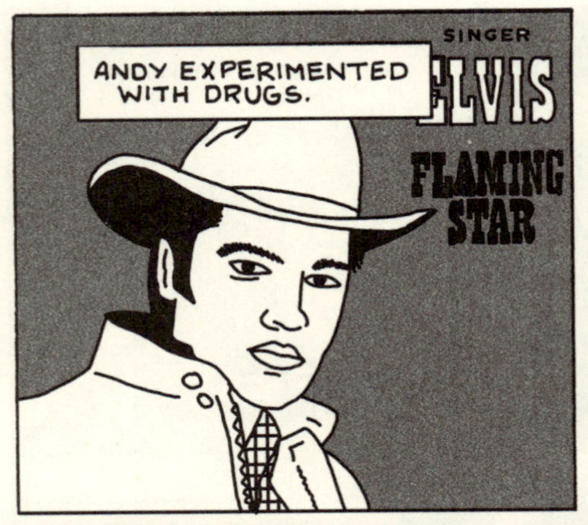
ANDY EXPERIMENTED WITH DRUGS.
SINGER
FLAMING STAR

WEED EVERY DAY.
FLAMING STAR

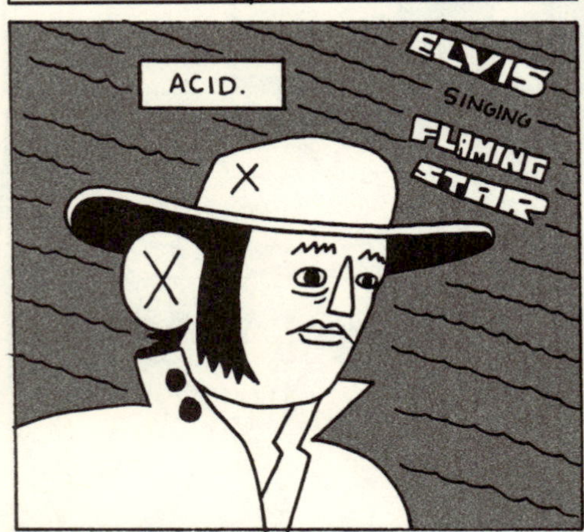
ACID.
ELVIS
SINGING
FLAMING
STAR

DMT.

DEXEDRINE.

HEY, KID! YOU GONNA BUY THAT RECORD?!
HUH??

ANDY WASN'T REALLY INTO HIGH SCHOOL.

HE GOT INTO PLAYING HOOKY AND GOING TO THE VILLAGE.

HE SEARCHED OUT BABATUNDE OLATUNJI.
JAZZ
DRUM

IS THAT HIM?
IT IS!

HELLO, MR. OLATUNJI, SIR. MY NAME IS ANDY KAUFMAN. YOU CAME TO MY SCHOOL AND SHOWED US YOUR DRUMS AND THEN I EVEN GOT MY OWN DRUMS AND I GOT YOUR RECORD AND TRIED TO PLAY IT BUT I'M NOT NEARLY AS GOOD AS YOU ARE. WOULD YOU EVER CONSIDER MAYBE TEACHING ME? OR I COULD BE YOUR APPRENTICE??
HUH?
JAZZ

I DON'T EVEN KNOW IF I'M HOLDING MY HANDS RIGHT. I CAN PAY YOU!

I... UH?
EVENTUALLY, HE SHOWED HIM A FEW THINGS.

WHAT WILL HAPPEN IF I TELL MY TEACHER I HATE HER?

SHE WILL SEND ME TO THE OFFICE...

THAT IS ALL.

BUT AT THE MID-SOUTH COLISEUM, ANDY'S FUTURE RIVAL, JERRY LAWLER, WAS A TEENAGE FAN LIKE HIM.

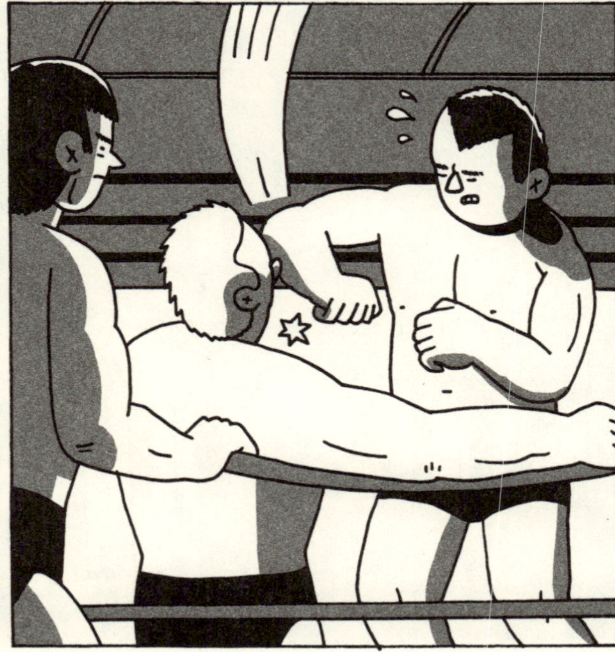

A FEW WEEKS LATER HE HEARD LEGENDARY MEMPHIS ANNOUNCER LANCE RUSSELL SAY:

LOCAL ARTIST JERRY LAWLER SENT US THESE AMAZING PIECES OF ART!

JERRY STARTED SENDING IN ART REGULARLY.
SPUTNIK
Monroe
Jerry Lawler
Jerry Lawler

HE WAS A FAN OF THE BAD GUYS.

The Infernos

JL

JUST LIKE ANDY.

JL

THEY EVEN BROUGHT JERRY ON TV TO SHOW OFF HIS ARTWORK.

LANCE TOOK JERRY AROUND TO MEET THE WRESTLERS.

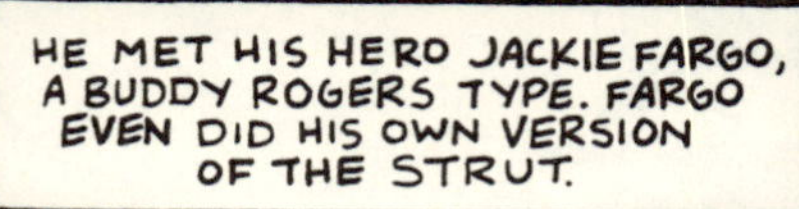
HE MET HIS HERO JACKIE FARGO, A BUDDY ROGERS TYPE. FARGO EVEN DID HIS OWN VERSION OF THE STRUT.

STRUT

AND TOGETHER LAWLER AND FARGO STARTED A SIGN-MAKING COMPANY.
LIVE MUSIC

DESPITE WORKING CLOSELY WITH FARGO, NO ONE EVER "SMARTENED HIM UP." AT THE TIME THE TRUE NATURE OF THE WRESTLING BUSINESS WAS A TIGHT SECRET, GUARDED AT ALL COSTS.
LOOKING GOOD, KID!

ONE NIGHT A CONCESSIONS WORKER SMARTENED JERRY UP...
HEY, KID!!

THESE GUYS ALL PLAN THESE MATCHES BEFOREHAND.
GET OUT! HOW D'YOU KNOW??

I'M SERIOUS! YOU WANNA SEE FOR YOURSELF?
LET'S GO!

YEAH, MAN, IT'S ALL A BIG FIX!

DROPKICK INTO THE PILEDRIVER INTO THE FINISH... FIFTEEN MINUTES.

KA-BOOM

ONE DAY WHILE WORKING AT THE SIGN COMPANY.
KNOCK KNOCK
HUH?

I'M LOOKING FOR JACKIE FARGO.
I'M A WRESTLER.

HE'S NOT HERE RIGHT NOW.

HEY, THIS GUY IS ONLY A FEW YEARS OLDER THAN ME. HE'S A WRESTLER? HOW'D HE GET IN?

HEY, MAN, WAIT UP!

I'M LOOKING TO GET INTO WRESTLING MYSELF. CAN YOU HELP ME OUT?

THIS GUY WAS ABOUT TO GIVE JERRY A LESSON ON THE WRESTLING BUSINESS BY SCAMMING HIM OUT OF SEVENTY-FIVE BUCKS.
WELL, KID, FIRST THING...
YOU'RE GONNA NEED A GOOD PAIR OF BOOTS.

PAIR OF TRUNKS TOO... YOU GOT ANY OF THOSE??

NO! I DON'T EVEN KNOW WHERE TO GET 'EM!!

I GOT SOME EXTRAS HERE... GUESS I COULD DO YOU A FAVOR AND SELL 'EM TO YOU.

REALLY!? YOU'D DO THAT!?

YEAH, NO PROBLEM SEVENTY-FIVE BUCKS EACH -- CHEAP!

GREAT!!

TO WRESTLERS AT THE TIME, EVERYONE WAS A SUCKER. THERE WAS A BARRIER TO ENTRY. THIS WAS A SECRET SOCIETY.

IN THIS ERA IT WAS IMPORTANT TO BUSINESS THAT PEOPLE TRULY BOUGHT INTO WRESTLING AS A SPORT.

THE AUDIENCE NEEDED TO BELIEVE NOT JUST THAT THEY WERE SEEING A REAL FIGHT...

...BUT THAT WRESTLERS WERE REAL CHARACTERS WITH REAL MOTIVATIONS.

EVERYONE WHO KNEW THE TRUTH KEPT THE SECRET CLOSELY GUARDED. LIKE THE CODE OF MAGICIANS.

IF THEY LET SOME UNVETTED PUNK IN ON ALL THE SECRETS...
RING THE BELL!!

HE COULD DESTROY THE BUSINESS FOR EVERYONE.

EVEN WITH TIGHTS, BOOTS, AND AN INTRODUCTION, THE PROMOTER WOULDN'T LET JERRY WORK WITHOUT EXPERIENCE.

WELL, I WORKED IN FLORIDA.

OH, YOU WORKED IN FLORIDA, HUH? WELL, THEN WHO IS THE PROMOTER RUNNING THE SHOW DOWN THERE IN FLORIDA?

UH??

SORRY.
GET LOST, KID.

I JUST THOUGHT IF I WRESTLED THEN I COULD TALK ABOUT IT ON MY RADIO SHOW.

WELL, NOW, WAIT A MINUTE! DID YOU SAY YOU HAD A RADIO SHOW??

THE PROMOTER LET JERRY GET UP THERE AND HAVE A MATCH, BUT DIDN'T REALLY TEACH HIM ANYTHING.

AVON THEATRE
WEST MEMPHIS, AR

AVON
WRESTLING

JERRY GOT A BIG IDEA FOR A MOVE IN THE RING. SOMETHING HE SAW BEFORE THAT WOULD LOOK REALLY COOL.

THROW ME AGAINST THE ROPES...
THEN OUT OF THE RING.

PFFT... YOU GOT IT, KID.

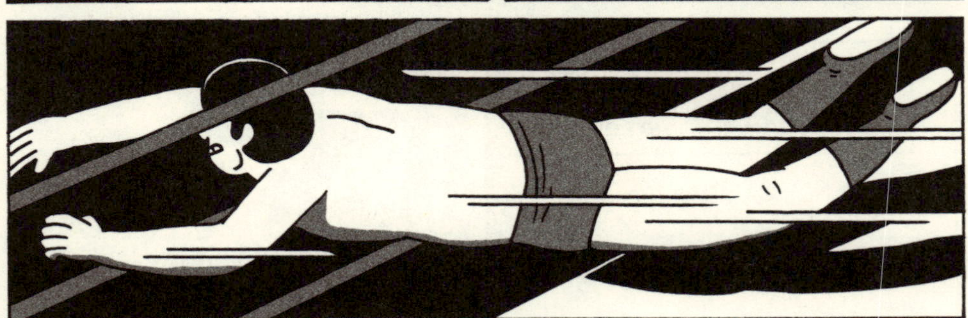

CRANG
CLASH
CLANG!!
CRONG
CLOPSH!

THE NEXT THING HE REMEMBERED WAS WAKING UP BACKSTAGE.

SPROING!!

GIVE HIM AIR!!

FAN THE KID!

AHH, HE'S FINE!!

JERRY HAD FOUND HIS CALLING IN LIFE.

MEANWHILE...

ANDY'S DAD CONVINCED HIM TO ATTEND JUNIOR COLLEGE IN BOSTON AFTER HIGH SCHOOL.

ONE NIGHT HE AND HIS HIPPIE FRIENDS WENT TO A BAR IN THE WRONG PART OF TOWN.
BEAT IT, FREAK!
STAY OUT, HIPPIE!

I'M SORRY!

I SWEAR I'LL GET A HAIRCUT TOMORROW!

SOON AFTER, ANDY MADE A CHANGE.
THIS IS MY LAST JOINT EVER, MAN. I'M SERIOUS.
ARE YOU FOR REAL?? NO WAY...
BUT HE WAS SERIOUS.

ANDY HAD DISCOVERED TRANSCENDENTAL MEDITATION, AND IT REQUIRED HIM TO QUIT ALCOHOL AND DRUGS.

HE'D BECOME MORE IN-TUNE WITH HIS TRUE SELF.

If we think of defeat
that's what we get;
If we're undecided, then
nothing will happen for us.
We must just pick something
great to do and do it.
Never think of failure at
all. For as we think now,
that's what we get.
- Maharishi Mahesh Yogi

ANDY'S DAILY MANTRA

HE KNEW HE WAS A TRULY UNIQUE TYPE OF PEFORMER,

AND HE KNEW HE LOVED ELVIS.

I'M UNCLE ANDY, I'M UNCLE ANDY!

WE'RE GONNA HAVE A LOT OF FUN TODAY!

THE CHARACTERS WERE ALL EXAGGERATED AND WACKY!

ANDY PLAYED EACH WITH A UNIQUE VIGOR!

I AM THE GREATEST!

ANDY DID MEET ELVIS.

HE MADE A PLAN HE KNEW HE COULD EXECUTE.

ELVIS WAS PLAYING A SERIES OF SHOWS AT THE INTERNATIONAL HOTEL IN LAS VEGAS.

INTE
INTERNATIONAL
ELVIS
EXCITING

ELVIS
I ♡
I ♡ Elvis

ANDY WAS THERE TO SEE THE KING, BUT HE HAPPENED UPON SOMEONE ELSE.

SOME OLD LOUNGE SINGER. A KIND OF HEINOUS GUY. DRUNK. NOT EVEN A GOOD SINGER REALLY. HE MIGHT'VE BEEN A GREAT ENTERTAINER ONCE, BUT HE WASN'T TONIGHT.
ANDY CALLED HIM TONY CLIFTON.

THIS IS YOUR WIFE!?
HAW!

SIR! YOU ARE SPILLING YOUR DRINK!!

THIS GUY DOESN'T CARE AT ALL! THE CROWD HATES HIM!
DAMN!

IMPRESSIVE.

HEY, MISTER, DO YOU KNOW IF ELVIS COMES THROUGH HERE? THIS WAY?
I REALLY GOTTA MEET ELVIS...
GOD

HUH?
WHAT?

SEE, I WROTE THIS BOOK ABOUT ELVIS AND I WANNA SHOW IT TO HIM. I'M GONNA BE A STAR LIKE HIM ONE DAY AND I NEED HIS BLESSING.

YOU WROTE THIS?

YUP.

ANDY COULD LAY ON THIS INNOCENT CHILD ACT.
YOU JUST WANT TO SHOW HIM YOUR BOOK?
LIKE A POOR BABE IN THE WOODS.
THAT'S ALL?

OK, KID, LISTEN: AFTER THE SHOW HE COMES THROUGH THIS KITCHEN. USUALLY RIGHT AROUND 12:30. GOOD LUCK!

HE FOUND A KITCHEN PANTRY TO WAIT FOR THE KING.

HE HAD TO WAIT A FEW HOURS. TO KILL TIME HE SAID HIS MEDITATIVE CHANTS.
...

HE ALSO HAD TIME TO THINK ABOUT THAT LOUNGE SINGER...TONY CLIFTON.
HAHA

FINALLY, HE HEARD THE KING'S VOICE IN THE DISTANCE. IT WAS UNMISTAKABLE.

great show
tonight.

MR. PRESLEY, NICE TO MEET YOU. MY NAME IS ANDY KAUFMAN. I WROTE THIS BOOK ABOUT YOU. I WANTED TO SHOW YOU.
GOD

YOU WROTE THIS?
YEAH! IT'S ABOUT YOU AND I'M GONNA BE FAMOUS LIKE YOU ONE DAY...

THAT'S VERY GOOD!
VERY GOOD!

AS THEY WALKED AWAY ANDY WAS ELATED EVEN AS HE HEARD...

MAN, THAT GUY WAS WEIRD!

HELL'S KITCHEN, NY

ANDY STAYED IN CHARACTER EVEN OFFSTAGE.

THIS WAS SOMETHING HE PICKED UP FROM WRESTLING.

HE'D PERFORM IN HIS GRANDPA'S OLD COAT.

OWERS BY Richard

IMPROV COMEDY CLUB

IMPROV COMEDY CLUB

it is ok for me to bring this in here?*

SURE.

BUDD FRIEDMAN, OWNER OF THE IMPROV

HIS MONOCLE

*IN HIS FICTIONAL ACCENT

BOB ZMUDA, LOCAL YOUNG COMEDIAN
EXIT
IS THIS GUY FOR REAL? WHAT'S WITH ALL THESE PROPS?
I GUESS WE'LL SEE.
WHERE YOU FROM? I'LL ANNOUNCE IT.
i am from a small island called Caspiar. i am nervous. it is my first time on stage.
"FOREIGN MAN" DISARMED THE AUDIENCE AND CREATED A STRANGE TENSION IN THE ROOM.
WAS THIS GUY FOR REAL?

CRACKLY...

COUGH

HERE I COME TO SAVE THE DAY!!

THIS CONCEPT OF ONLY PANTOMIMING ONE LINE FROM THE FAMILIAR CARTOON SONG SLAYED THE AUDIENCE.

BUT STILL KEPT THEM IN THE DARK ABOUT ANDY'S TRUE PERSONA.

HIS CRYING WOULD GET MORE AND MORE RHYTHMIC.

BABA-BOOEY-BABA-EEEEE

BWABA-BABA-EEE-EE-EE

BABBA-WABBA-EEE-EEE

BA-WA

BA-BA

EE-EE

BABA

EE-EE

SUDDENLY, HIS CRYING TURNS INTO A CONGA JAM.
JUST WHEN THE AUDIENCE WAS READY TO BELIEVE THIS MAN WAS A LEGITIMATE BUFFOON...
HE REVEALS A SPECTACULAR SKILL!
BOMBOH
BOBBA
BOBBA
HEE-EEE
BOBBA
EEE-EEE
BOBBUH
BOMBAH
EE-EE
EE-EEE
EE-EEE
EEE-EEE

thank you very much.

THEN HE'D BRING THE AUDIENCE BACK DOWN WITH SOME INCOMPETENT IMPRESSIONS.

now i will do an impression of johnny carson.
hello. i am johnny carson.

and now i will try another.
president richard nixon.

hello. i am richard nixon.
IMPR

IT WENT ON LIKE THIS.
IT GOT ~~A LITTLE~~ ANNOYING.

now i will imitate for you the elvis presley.

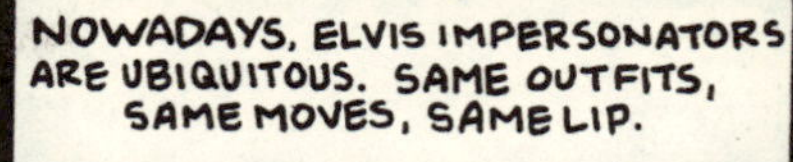
NOWADAYS, ELVIS IMPERSONATORS ARE UBIQUITOUS. SAME OUTFITS, SAME MOVES, SAME LIP.

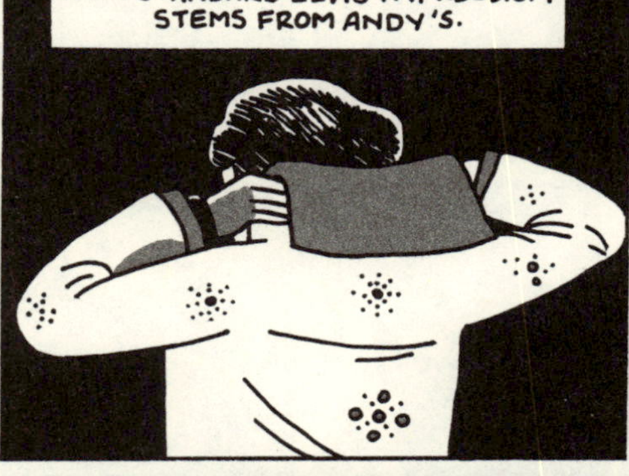
A LOT OF WHAT PEOPLE TODAY SEE AS A STANDARD ELVIS IMPRESSION STEMS FROM ANDY'S.

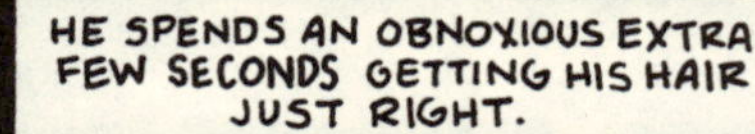
HE SPENDS AN OBNOXIOUS EXTRA FEW SECONDS GETTING HIS HAIR JUST RIGHT.

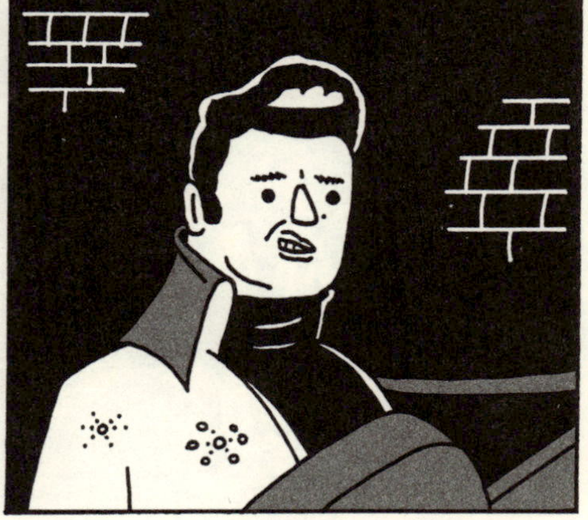

ANDY'S SPOT-ON ELVIS KNOCKED 'EM DEAD.

THIS WHOLE FABRICATION AND PERFORMANCE WAS UNLIKE ANYTHING PEOPLE HAD SEEN IN A COMEDY CLUB.

THE SHOW HAD BEEN PERFORMED A MILLION TIMES IN ANDY'S BASEMENT.

thank you very much.

BUDD FRIEDMAN AND BOB ZMUDA WERE STRUCK DUMB. THEY'D BEEN HAD, JUST LIKE THE REST OF THE AUDIENCE.
POP
HA HA
HA HA
HA
HA HA
HEY, MAN, LEMME HELP YOU WITH THAT. 
I'M BOB.
BOB ZMUDA QUICKLY INGRATIATED HIMSELF TO ANDY AND BECAME HIS FRIEND, SIDEKICK, AND WRITING PARTNER.

BOB ZMUDA AND ANDY BONDED OVER THE CONCEPT OF FUCKING WITH PEOPLE'S REALITY.
SO, WE'D JUST GO TO THE ZOO, Y'KNOW?
HAHA, YEAH?

BOB CAME FROM THE COUNTER-CULTURE MOVEMENT. HE'D JUST GO OUT AND CAUSE A STIR.
ALL OF A SUDDEN, AT THE SAME TIME A FEW OF US WOULD JUST GO:

"LION!! THE LION ESCAPED!!" AND THEN RUN AWAY SCARED.

THE PEOPLE WERE FLIPPING OUT! JUST COMPLETELY FREAKING OUT! I ALMOST GOT ARRESTED!
ANDY LOVED IT.
HAHAHA!

BUT HE WAS ACTUALLY SAYING TRUE THINGS ABOUT HIMSELF AS ELVIS.

WELL...

I DO SOMETHING CALLED YOGA... AND TRANSCENDENTAL MEDITATION. IT HELPS ME A LOT.

HE STILL DID STAND-UP IN BOSTON, NEW YORK, AND LOS ANGELES. BUT HE WAS ALSO POPPING UP ON TV SETS ALL OVER.

THE DEAN MARTIN COMEDY WORLD, HOSTED BY JACKIE COOPER AND NIPSEY RUSSELL

THE JOE FRANKLIN SHOW

MONTY HALL'S VARIETY HOUR

THE LISA HARTMAN SHOW

REMEMBER JERRY LAWLER? HE FOUND HIMSELF ON TV IN MEMPHIS...

...THROWING A FIREBALL INTO HIS HERO JACKIE FARGO'S FACE.

HE'D LIGHT THE FLASH PAPER WITH A LIGHTER THAT WAS CONCEALED IN HIS TRUNKS...

...AND THEN UNLEASH THE BRIGHT BUT NOT-SO-HOT FLASH!!

OF COURSE, YOU DON'T GO STRAIGHT FROM BORROWING TRUNKS IN THE PARKING LOT DIRECTLY TO USING PYROTECHNICS ON TV.

WRESTLING HAD MANY INITIATION RITUALS MEANT TO KEEP OUT THE FLY-BY-NIGHTERS.

"TOJO YAMAMOTO" TOOK ADVANTAGE OF THE PUBLIC'S DISCOMFORT AROUND FOREIGNERS IN POST-WWII AMERICA, KIND OF LIKE FOREIGN MAN.

HE WAS AN ANGRY GUY AND ENJOYED TEACHING NEWCOMERS A LESSON WHILE APPEARING MENACING.

HE'D WORK "STIFF," LAYING IN CHOPS AND KICKS INSTEAD OF PULLING PUNCHES.

HE WAS DEVASTATING.

*PRO WRESTLING SLANG; DESCRIBES THE ACT OF MAKING WRESTLING BELIEVABLE TO THE AUDIENCE, USUALLY BY PRETENDING TO BE HURT.

JERRY'S TALENT FOR SELLING AND MAKING OTHER, MORE POPULAR WRESTLERS LOOK GOOD DIDN'T GO UNNOTICED BY BOOKERS.

HE BOUNCED AROUND THE RING LIKE A RED RUBBER BALL.

HE WENT UP AGAINST BIGGER DRAWS LIKE BOBO BRAZIL.

HE WRESTLED NWA CHAMP JACK BRISCO IN FRONT OF A SOLD-OUT CROWD OF 11,000.

JERRY WAS FAKING HIS WAY THROUGH AND LEARNING ON THE JOB.

UNTIL ONE DAY HE WASN'T FAKING IT ANYMORE.

HE WAS ON TV EVERY WEEK...

TALKING PEOPLE INTO THE BUILDING AND SELLING OUT THE MID-SOUTH COLISEUM REGULARLY.
SOLD OUT

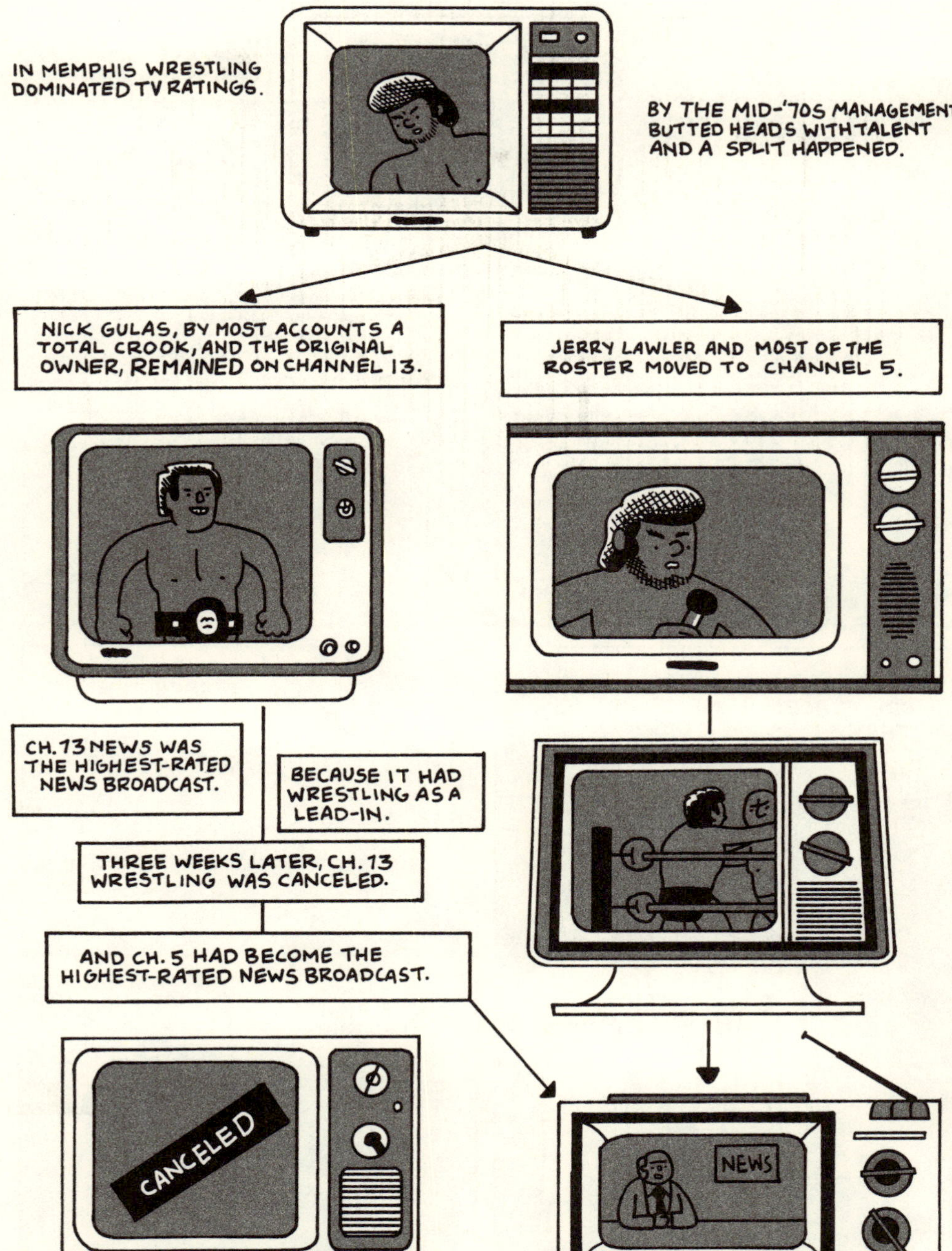
IN MEMPHIS WRESTLING DOMINATED TV RATINGS.
BY THE MID-'70S MANAGEMENT BUTTED HEADS WITH TALENT AND A SPLIT HAPPENED.
NICK GULAS, BY MOST ACCOUNTS A TOTAL CROOK, AND THE ORIGINAL OWNER, REMAINED ON CHANNEL 13.
JERRY LAWLER AND MOST OF THE ROSTER MOVED TO CHANNEL 5.
CH. 13 NEWS WAS THE HIGHEST-RATED NEWS BROADCAST.
BECAUSE IT HAD WRESTLING AS A LEAD-IN.
THREE WEEKS LATER, CH. 13 WRESTLING WAS CANCELED.
AND CH. 5 HAD BECOME THE HIGHEST-RATED NEWS BROADCAST.
CANCELED
NEWS

IT WAS ON TV DURING AN INTERVIEW THAT JERRY RECEIVED HIS "KING" MONIKER. THESE PROMOS WERE IMPROVISED JUST LIKE A LOT OF WHAT ANDY DID AT THE IMPROV THEATER.

LISTEN UP, FARGO! YOU'VE BEEN AROUND SO LONG YOU THINK YOU'RE THE KING!

WELL, THERE'S ONLY ONE KING IN MEMPHIS AND IT AIN'T YOU!!

JERRY CALLED ANOTHER WRESTLER NAMED "KING" BOBBY SHANE TO FIND OUT WHERE HE GOT HIS ROBE AND CROWN.

ACTUALLY, I'M ABOUT TO DROP THE CHARACTER. YOU CAN COME GRAB THE GEAR.

WITH HIS ROYAL GARMENTS PROCURED, MEMPHIS HAD A NEW KING.

MEANWHILE...

ANDY DEVELOPED A CHARACTER BASED ON THAT OLD VEGAS LOUNGE SINGER HE CALLED TONY CLIFTON. ANDY LIFTED HIS WHOLE ACT!
I'M USED TO PLAYING BIG VENUES...
NOT THIS DUMP.

THE GUY WAS A REAL JERK. HE WAS LIKE BUDDY ROGERS, THE BAD-GUY WRESTLER, TRYING TO GET HEAT FROM THE CROWD.
HIT IT.

♫ TIE THAT YELLOW RIBBON 'ROUND THAT OLD OAK TREE ♪
♪ IT'S BEEN THREE LONG YEARS... ♫ DO YOU STILL WANT...

HEY! PIANO MAN SLOW DOWN!
I'M THE REAL STAR HERE!

THE TONY CLIFTON CHARACTER AND JERRY LAWLER'S KING CHARACTER WERE CUT FROM THE SAME CLOTH.

BOTH WANTED FANS TO HATE THEM.

THEY BOTH CAME UP WITH ELABORATE COSTUMES.

THEY PRESENTED THEIR PERSONAS AS ARROGANT BUT PHYSICALLY ACTED LIKE BUFFOONS.

THE ONLY DIFFERENCE WAS AFTER THE KING RANTED HE'D GET PUMMELED BY A GOOD GUY WHILE THE CROWD CHEERED.
CLIFTON'S CROWDS ONLY HOPED THIS WOULD HAPPEN.

ANDY ENDED UP PASSING THE CHARACTER ON TO HIS FRIEND AND COLLABORATOR BOB ZMUDA.

IT REQUIRED A LOT OF HOLLYWOOD MAKEUP.

FAKE TEETH

THE CONSTANT NEGATIVITY OF THE CHARACTER WAS ANTITHETICAL TO ANDY'S TRUE PEACEFUL NATURE.

BUT IT CLEARLY WORKED.

AFTER SEEING GORILLA MONSOON WHIP KILLER KOWALSKI IN FRONT OF 22,000 FANS, ANDY WAS HOOKED AGAIN.

WRESTLING HADN'T CHANGED SINCE HIS YOUTH, BUT ANDY WAS NOW VIEWING IT IN A NEW LIGHT.

THESE MEN WEREN'T FIGHTING. THEY WERE PERFORMING.

THEY WEREN'T ADVERSARIES. THEY WERE DANCE PARTNERS MANIPULATING A CROWD.
CHOMP

BUT THE WRESTLING CROWD WASN'T ASKING ITSELF, "IS THIS GUY FOR REAL?" THE WAY THE THE COMEDY CLUB FANS DID.
THEY WERE ACCEPTING THAT GORILLA MONSOON WAS BLEEDING FROM BEING BITTEN, NOT FROM A WELL-CONCEALED BLADE.

HIS AUDITION WAS HIM RECITING THE SONG "MACARTHUR PARK"'S NOTORIOUSLY SILLY LYRICS IN A COMPLETELY DEADPAN MANNER.

ON THE SERIES PREMIER OF NBC'S "SATURDAY NIGHT LIVE," ANDY DID HIS "MIGHTY MOUSE" ROUTINE. HE'D BECOME A REGULAR GUEST, BUT NOT A FULL-TIME CAST MEMBER.

FINAL ★★★★ DAILY NEWS

Vol. 59 New York, Wednesday, August 1977 Price: 20 cents

ELVIS PRESLEY DIES AT 42

Singer Suffers Heart Attack

Berkowitz Pleads Innocent; Plans Insanity Defense

Report: Carter Picks Ala. Judge as FBI Chief

MAHARISHI MAHESH YOGI SAID:
"WE MUST TAKE SITUATIONS AS THEY ARE. WE MUST ONLY CHANGE OUR MENTAL ATTITUDES TOWARDS THEM."
YOU ALL RIGHT, MAN?
YEAH.

WHEN ANDY PERFORMED FOREIGN MAN ON "SATURDAY NIGHT LIVE," HE MADE A POWERFUL FAN.

JAMES L. BROOKS, TV WRITER
WE NEED THIS GUY FOR "TAXI"!
HAW HAW!!
THANK YOU VERY MUCH.

SOON AFTER, BROOKS AND THE THREE OTHER "TAXI" CREATORS DESCENDED UPON THE COMEDY STORE.

*ANDY'S MANAGER, GEORGE SHAPIRO **ACTUALLY THAT NIGHT BOB ZMUDA WAS ON STAGE.

OK, ANDY, WE'VE GOT A NEW SHOW COMING TO ABC! IT'S CALLED "TAXI"! WE HAVE THIS IDEA FOR YOU TO PLAY A FOREIGN TAXI MECHANIC! CHECK IT OUT! YOU'RE GONNA LOVE THE NAME: LATKA GRAVAS!
NO ADMITTANCE

YOU MEAN FOREIGN MAN?
YES!! WE LOVE FOREIGN MAN!
PR

AND WE ABSOLUTELY LOVE TONY CLIFTON!!

UMEDY
COM
YOU LOVE TONY CLIFTON? THAT GUY IS AN ASSHOLE.
ORE
STO

WAS NOT THRILLED WITH THE IDEA THAT THE NETWORK WOUL
N HIS FOREIGN MAN CHARACTER.

WOULD NO LONGER BE HIS.

T PRIME-TIME TV?? THIS WAS MAJOR FAME.

DY KAUFMAN" WOULD BECOME A HOUSEHOLD NAME.

TOOK THE JOB. BUT HE MADE THEM ALSO HIRE TONY CLIFTON
R A FEW EPISODES.

IFTON WAS QUICKLY FIRED.

REALITY IT WAS ANDY IN DISGUISE.

ONE DAY:

WHAT THE HELL EVEN IS THIS THING?!

8MM FILM PLAYER

LOOK THROUGH THE VIEWFINDER AND TURN THE CRANK. IT'S SUPER-HOT TO ME...

IT WAS A SHORT MOVIE OF TWO WOMEN WRESTLING. THEY WEREN'T REALLY SEXUAL AT ALL. REGULAR WRESTLING IN REGULAR J.C. PENNEY UNDERPANTS.

ANDY HAD READ IN AN UNAUTHORIZED BIOGRAPHY THAT THIS WAS SOMETHING ELVIS LIKED AND HAD SOUGHT IT OUT.

NOW BOB KNEW JUST WHAT TO GET ANDY FOR HIS BIRTHDAY.

EVERYONE CLEAR THE FLOOR! IT'S TIME FOR THE SURPRISE!

ANDY, YOU SIT RIGHT THERE...
NOW THE MAIN EVENT!

MARILYN!
VERSUS GAIL!

I AM THE GREATEST!

SAY "UNCLE"!
SAY "UNCLE"!
NEVER!

THAT WAS A GREAT MATCH, MARILYN.
THANKS.

MAYBE AFTER THE PARTY WE CAN WRESTLE.
SURE. YOU THINK YOU CAN BEAT ME?

EVERYONE OUT! PARTY'S OVER!

THEY'D WRESTLE, THEN SCREW.

THIS WOULD BECOME ONE OF ANDY'S REGULAR SEXUAL PROCLIVITIES.

BOB! I FIGURED OUT HOW TO GET WRESTLING INTO THE ACT!

FIRST, I ONLY WRESTLE WOMEN. WE TELL THE COLLEGE BEFOREHAND THAT ANY WOMAN WHO CAN PIN ME WILL GET $500! JUST LIKE OLD CARNIVAL-STYLE WRESTLING.

AND I'LL JUST BE A COMPLETE PIG. A CHAUVINIST SHIT HEEL.
JUST LIKE CLIFTON BUT LIKE BUDDY ROGERS, TOO.

OH MAN, THE WOMEN'S LIBBERS ARE GONNA GO COMPLETELY APESHIT.

HAHA! I'LL BE TOTALLY HATED!
MWA-HA-HA-HAW

AND I BET I SCORE WITH LIKE 80% OF THE CHICKS.

COLORADO STATE UNIVERSITY • FEBRUARY 10 AND 11

WRESTLE

ANDY KAUFMAN

LADIES ONLY

7PM / THE GYM

WIN $500

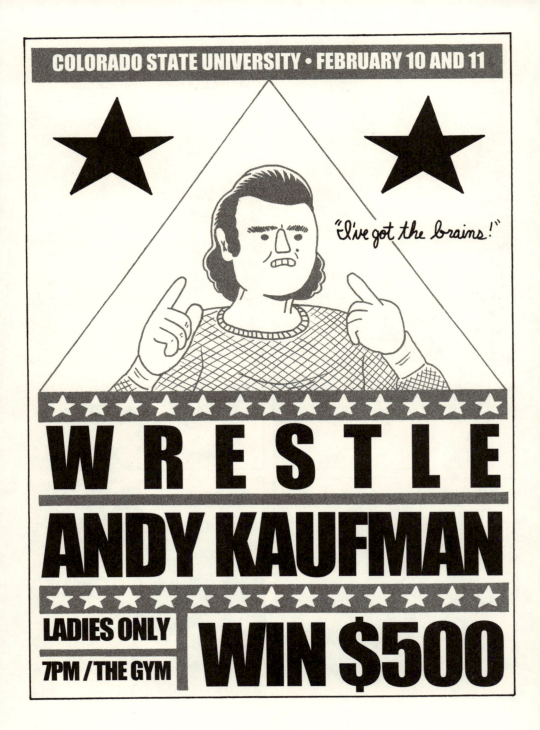

WOMEN ARE DUMB! THEY BELONG IN THE KITCHEN!
I'VE GOT THE BRAINS! I CAN'T BE PINNED!!

GO!
FIGHT!

HOW ABOUT YOU COME MEET ME AFTER THE SHOW?
EWW! UP YOURS!

ANDY WAS A COMPETENT AMATEUR WRESTLER AND COULDN'T BE PINNED.

BRING OUT A NEW CHALLENGER!!
COME ON!
COWARD!

HOW ABOUT WE WRESTLE LATER IN MY DRESSING ROOM?
YOU MEAN IT? FOR REAL??

ANDY'S WRESTLING GEAR WAS DESIGNED TO CAMOUFLAGE AROUSAL.

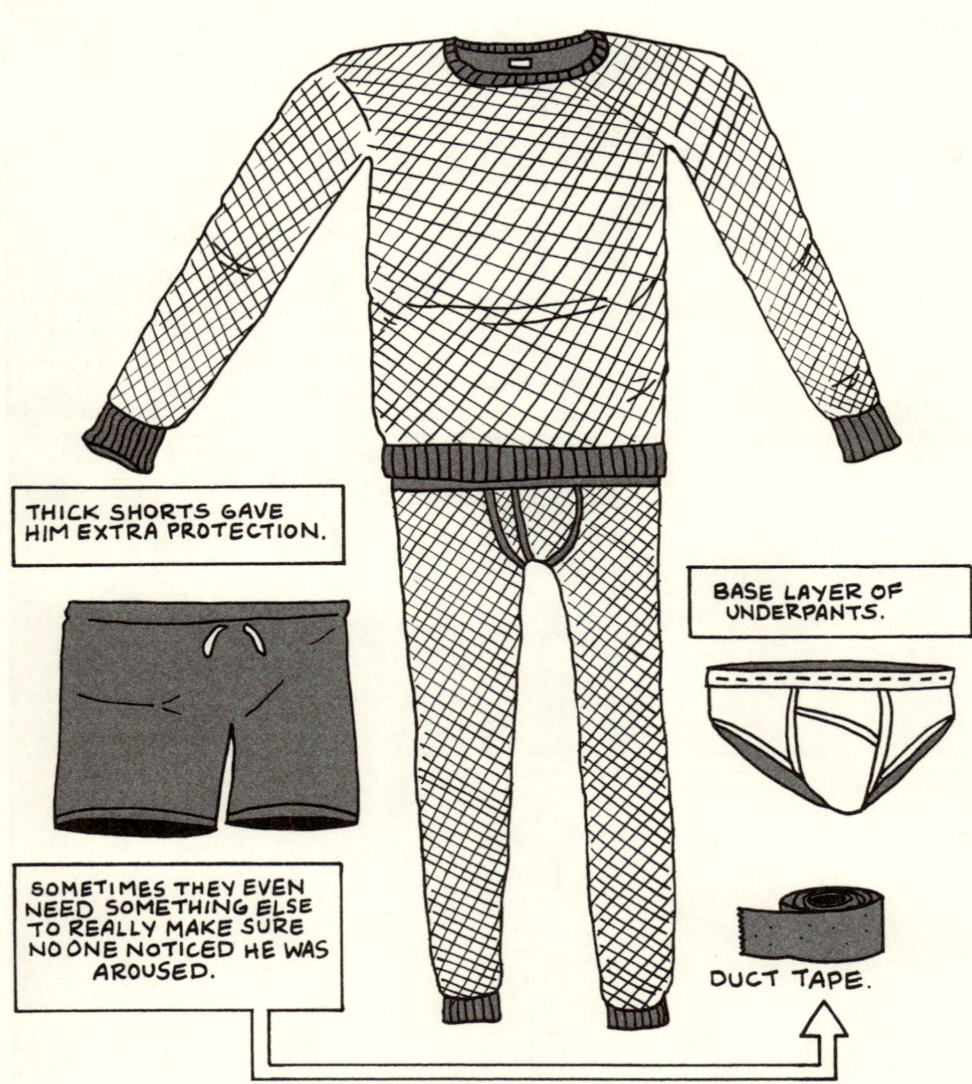

THE ACT KEPT DEVELOPING AND ANDY SOON DECLARED HIMSELF:

I'M HERE TONIGHT TO WRESTLE!!

IF ANY WOMAN CAN PIN ME, THEY'LL GET $1,000!!

THIS IS REAL!!

THIS IS NOT A COMEDY ACT!!

HE TOOK ON ALL COMERS AND TOOK IT SERIOUSLY.

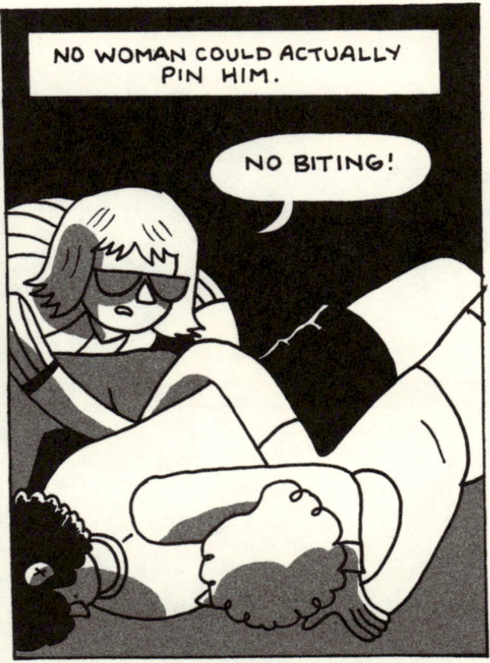
NO WOMAN COULD ACTUALLY PIN HIM.
NO BITING!

EVEN AS RUMORS OF HIS ACT SPREAD AND HIS OPPONENTS GOT TOUGHER.
ONE, TWO, THREE!

ANDY KEPT WINNING. THE MATCHES WERE NOT FIXED. THEY WERE REAL AMATEUR WRESTLING MATCHES.

DURING THE TOUR, BOB AND ANDY TOOK A DETOUR TO MEMPHIS TO CHECK OUT GRACELAND.
I'VE GOT A MILLION-DOLLAR IDEA.

A NIGHTCLUB WHERE MEN AND WOMEN WRESTLE EACH OTHER!

IT'S WAY MORE SEXUAL THAN DANCING, SERIOUSLY!

ONCE YOU BREAK THE TOUCH BARRIER IN THE SPIRIT OF COMPETITION?
EVERYONE WOULD GET LAID EVERY NIGHT!

THEY FINALLY ROLLED UP AT GRACELAND. ELVIS'S HOME.
THE PLACE WHERE HE DIED.
THEY EVEN GOT A SPECIAL TOUR.

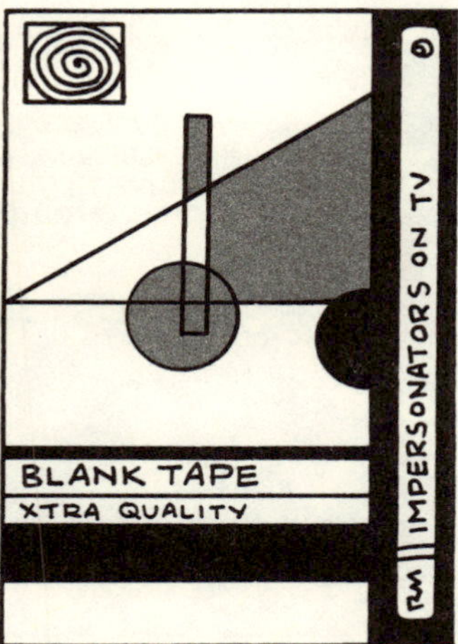

HE EVEN SNUCK INTO THE ACTUAL BATHROOM WHERE ELVIS EXPIRED AND USED IT.

WHAT ELSE IS THERE IN LIFE?

NEWS

ACTOR KAUFMAN DROPS DEAD

HAHAHAHA

I COULD PULL IT OFF!!

1980: LOS ANGELES GRAND OLYMPIC AUDITORIUM

IT WASN'T PURELY ABOUT SEX FOR ANDY.

BOXING TUES. WRESTLING

Olympic

THIS WAS THEATER-IN-THE-ROUND...

BOOO B

UP YOU

BOOO

BOO

OH MY GOD!!
IT'S "CLASSY" FREDDIE BLASSIE!

FROM WHEN I WAS A KID!!
HE'S STILL SO AWESOME!

HE'S GOT SO MUCH FLASH! SO MUCH PIZZAZZ! HE'S LIKE ELVIS!

... BUT BETTER!

I AM THE, THE, THE GREATEST WRESTLER OF ALL TIME! WOMEN SWOON OVER ME! EVEN THE PIGS IN THIS PLACE!
THE MEN HERE, TOO! YOU'RE A BUNCH OF PENCIL-NECK GEEKS!!!
YEAH! THAT'S RIGHT!! ALL OF YOU PUNKS ARE SCUM-SUCKING...
NAIL-BITING!
GLUE-SNIFFING!
BOOT-LICKING!
GUT-GRINDING!
DIRTY, LOUSY, ROTTEN, STINKING FREAKS!!
I'M A WINNER AND PEOPLE LOVE A WINNER AND THEY HATE A LOSER!
YOU'RE ALL LOSERS!!
YOU BUNCHA PENCIL-NECK GEEKS!

LOCKER ROOM
ANDY COULDN'T HELP IT. HE HAD TO GO BACKSTAGE AND FIND FREDDIE BLASSIE.
TOLOS

HEY!
HEY! YOU CAN'T BE BACK HERE!

OH! I'M SORRY, SIR! SORRY. SORRY.
I WAS JUST LOOKING FOR MR. BLASSIE, KING OF MEN.

HEY! YOU'RE THAT GUY FROM "TAXI"!!
OMG

HAHA! YOU'RE HILARIOUS! THE LOCKER ROOM IS RIGHT BACK OVER THAT WAY.
COOL.

HEY, I...

YOU'RE NOT ALLOWED BACK HERE!!

NO, SEE... IT'S OK... I'M ANDY... A HUGE FAN...

GET THE HELL OUT BEFORE I BITE YOUR FUCKING FACE OFF!!
YOU DAMN NUT!!

*"KAYFABE" IS A CODE WORD FOR WRESTLING LAW. IT MEANS ONE MUST KEEP THE REALITY OF THE WRESTLING BUSINESS A TOTAL SECRET.

MR. BLASSIE, MY NAME IS ANDY KAUFMAN. I'M A COMEDIAN AND I JUST WANNA TALK ABOUT WRESTLING!!

WHAT EXACTLY DO YOU WANT, KID?

DANNY'S

GRAB THEM CAKES

YOU'RE OUT THERE AND YOU'RE A SHINING STAR...
YOU'RE THE KING OUT THERE. YOU'RE ELVIS!

YOU'VE ALWAYS GOT THE PERFECT LINE.
LIKE AT ANY GIVEN MOMENT... READY TO GO!

YOU DON'T EVEN NEED A SPOTLIGHT, MR. BLASSIE.

BLASSIE HAD A DISTANT RELATIONSHIP WITH HIS OWN KIDS. A PRO WRESTLER'S SCHEDULE DOESN'T LEND ITSELF TO FATHERHOOD. HIS CHILDREN TREATED HIM WITH SCORN. HERE'S A FAMOUS TV STAR, SURE, BUT ALSO THIS INSECURE KID ADMIRING HIM.
SERIOUSLY!

NAH.
SHUT UP, KID.

ANDY BEGAN SNEAKING BACKSTAGE AT WRESTLING SHOWS REGULARLY.

MADISON SQUARE GARDEN

MR. MCMAHON!

HUH?

MR. MCMAHON, I'VE BEEN WRESTLING IN MY ACT AND I THINK I'M READY TO WORK THE GARDEN.

VINCE MCMAHON, SR., WAS UNMOVED.
MR. KAUFMAN, WE'RE NOT INTERESTED. YOU'RE NOT EVEN ALLOWED BACK HERE.

DAD, YOU KNOW HE'S A HUGE CELEBRITY. IT WOULD BRING US LOTS OF MAINSTREAM ATTENTION!

NO. THAT'S NOT HOW IT WORKS. CELEBRITIES CHEAPEN OUR BUSINESS. WHO'S GONNA FEAR OUR ATHLETES IF THAT JACKASS IS CALLING HIMSELF A WRESTER??
DAMMIT, IT'D MAKE FOOLS OF US ALL!!

MR. KAUFMAN! WAIT UP!

LISTEN: MY DAD HAS HIS IDEAS ABOUT THIS BUSINESS... I CAN'T DO ANYTHING TO CHANGE THAT.
YOU CAN'T WRESTLE FOR US ON OUR CARDS.
WE JUST CAN'T HAVE IT.
I KNOW THAT'S WHAT YOU WANT.

BUT...
WE LIKE TO HIGHLIGHT CELEBRITIES IN OUR AUDIENCES AT LIVE EVENTS. HOW ABOUT AN INTERVIEW?

ON CAMERA?

ON CAMERA.

YOU MAY HAVE SEEN HIM ON "SATURDAY NIGHT LIVE" OR MAYBE YOU KNOW HIM AS LATKA FROM TV'S "TAXI."
A TRUE SUPERSTAR OF THE ENTERTAINMENT BUSINESS: MR. ANDY KAUFMAN.
MR. KAUFMAN, YOU DO SOME WRESTLING YOURSELF BUT JUST WITH THE LADIES.

OR THE MENTAL!
CHUCKLE

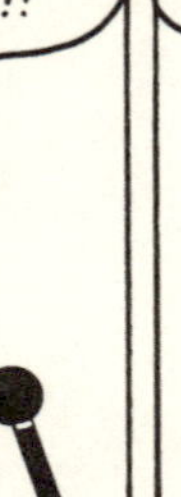

WRESTLING PHOTOGRAPHER AND MAGAZINE EDITOR BILL APTER WAS A BACKSTAGE MAINSTAY AT MSG.
HMMM

AS A KEEN OBSERVER, HE FELT VINCE, SR.'S DISCOMFORT WHEN ANDY WOULD TALK HIS EAR OFF.

ENJOY THE MATCHES.

LISTEN, BILL, SEE IF YOU CAN GET THIS MANIAC TO GO BACK TO HIS SEAT. HE'S A PAIN IN MY ASS.

HELLO, EXCUSE ME, MR. KAUFMAN. I'M BILL APTER...

FROM THE MAGAZINES?? OH MY GOD, REALLY??

YOU KNOW WHO I AM??

BILL APTER.

OH, HELLO, MR. KAUFMAN! SURE. I WOULD LOVE TO CHAT...

andy kaufman!

SURE, SURE, I'VE MET BUDDY ROGERS BEFORE...
SO COOL!!

MUCH LATER:
LISTEN, ANDY, I'M GONNA HAVE TO GET BACK TO WORK HERE...

ANDY SOON BROUGHT HIS WRESTLING ACT TO HIS LARGEST AUDIENCE:

"SATURDAY NIGHT LIVE"

HE DID THE SAME ACT HE'D BEEN DOING ON THE ROAD.

HE OFFERED $1,000 TO ANYONE WHO COULD BEAT HIM. THIS TIME ON NATIONAL TELEVISION!

BEFORE THE MATCH:

"SNL" MANAGER GEORGE SHAPIRO AND ANDY HIMSELF WERE FLOODED WITH HUNDREDS OF LETTERS FROM WOMEN WHO WANTED TO WRESTLE ANDY.
ROAR!
Linda
If I'm chosen you will need an ambulance to get home! -Vicki
aufman
860
ity Stat
New York, New Y
u're just a dog! I have
'm willing to bet that I
are trash!!
y Kaufman
ould easi
s's got n
m a 4th g
ill put you in your place
r place is the trash!
ouldn't treat my DOG the
I plan on treating you.
ill beat you!!
yours,
Michelle
Prepare You
Koffman
This farm girl will put you to sleep

Mr. Kauffman,
old 5'11"
h 136 lbs.
be toast!
ou are scum!
ll boil y
u're noth
t an assh
-Nancy
Kauffman
I Challenge you to a Real Fight!
- Rachel
f!
december '79
THEY WERE PLAYING RIGHT INTO HIS HANDS.
ate your
guts! I've got all the brains
anyone would need to beat
skinny butt!!!!! I am
ninth grade! only 14
still KICK your
UGLY FACE into outer

IS THIS BUDDY ROGERS? YOU DON'T KNOW ME BUT I HAVE IDOLIZED YOU FOR MANY YEARS. I WAS THERE WHEN THAT CHUMP BRUNO SAMMARTINO STOLE YOUR TITLE AND IT BROKE MY HEART. I STOPPED WATCHING FOR YEARS.
1 2 3
4 5 6
7 8 9
0 *

EVEN THOUGH WE'VE NEVER MET, I CONSIDER YOU A SPIRITUAL ADVISOR. I WOULD BE HUMBLED AND HONORED IF YOU WOULD BE IN MY CORNER WHEN I WRESTLE ON "SATURDAY NIGHT LIVE" ON THE 22ND.

IT WOULD BE ONLY A PARTIAL PAYBACK FOR THE YEARS OF PLEASURE AND INSPIRATION YOU'VE GIVEN ME. PLEASE SAY YOU WILL!!

WHO THE HELL IS THIS!!?

HOW GREAT IS BUDDY ROGERS, HUH, DICK?
EXIT→
DICK EBERSOL, NBC EXEC

YOU GOTTA GET BEHIND THIS STUFF, MAN. THESE GUYS ARE THE REAL DEAL! TRUE PERFORMERS!

IT'S GONNA GET BIG SOON. HUGE! I'M TELLING YOU!

NO, ANDY, COME ON. THIS IS LOWBROW STUFF.

IT'LL NEVER BE MAINSTREAM.

...TO PROVE WE'RE SERIOUS, "SNL," NOT US, CHOSE THE FOUR FINALISTS. THOSE FOUR CONTESTANTS WRESTLED ONE ANOTHER IN AN ELIMINATION TOURNAMENT AT THE LOCAL YMCA.
I, FORMER WORLD CHAMPION BUDDY ROGERS, HAVE BECOME ANDY KAUFMAN'S MANAGER.

ROGERS TRULY WASN'T READY FOR PRIME TIME. LORNE MICHAELS WANTED HIS PART CUT.

ZMUDA, TELL ANDY WE'RE PULLING BUDDY ROGERS. IT'S NOT PLAYING.
IT DOESN'T ADD ANYTHING.

BESIDES, WE NEED MORE ROOM FOR THE "MR. BILL" SKETCH.

ANDY IS GONNA PITCH A FIT. IT'S HIS HERO!!
SCREW IT. ANDY PAYS ME, NOT LORNE MICHAELS.

ZMUDA DIDN'T TELL ANDY ABOUT THE CUT UNTIL JUST PRIOR TO GOING LIVE.

BUDDY STUMBLED THROUGH HIS THREE-MINUTE SPEECH.

IT WAS NICE TO GET THE CHAMP ON TV.

NOTHING WAS EVER ENOUGH. ANDY WOULD STILL FIND HIS WAY INTO THE BOWELS OF MADISON SQUARE GARDEN REGULARLY.

HEY, WHERE ARE YOU HEADED?
JUST HOME TO MY PLACE IN QUEENS.

CAN I WALK WITH YOU AND TALK WRESTLING??
SURE.

DID YOU SEE I GOT BUDDY ROGERS ON "SATURDAY NIGHT LIVE"?

IT WAS GREAT, BUT IF I DID IT AGAIN I'D ASK FREDDIE.

BLASSIE SHINES OUT THERE. JUST LIKE ELVIS!
HA!

YOU THINK ELVIS REALLY STILL LIVES??
IT WOULD BE A DREAM IF IT WAS TRUE AND HE MADE A COMEBACK.
MET LIFE
I USED ELVIS'S TAILOR TO MAKE MY COSTUMES AND I ASKED HIM THE SAME QUESTION.
HE SAID: "NO ONE COULD EAT THAT MANY MONTE CRISTOS AND LIVE."
HAW!
WOULD BE A GREAT SCAM, THOUGH, HUH?

HEY, DO YOU REMEMBER THE KANGAROO BROTHERS?

THIS IS YOUR PLACE, HUH?

DO YOU WANNA COME UP?

BILL, I WAS DELIVERED SOME OF YOUR MAIL BY ACCIDENT--

WHAT THE HECK?! IS THAT THE GUY FROM FRICKIN' "TAXI"??

WRESTLIN
WRESTLING
WREST

WHOA! SO MANY WRESTLING MAGAZINES! YOU DO AMAZING WORK, BILL.

THERE'S GOTTA BE A WAY I CAN CONVINCE VINCE TO LET ME WRESTLE! C'MON, RIGHT??

WHAT DO I HAVE TO DO? LIFT WEIGHTS? PUMP IRON? GET BLOODY??

I CAN GET BLOODY!!

AN HOUR LATER:

DO YOU NERDS TALK ABOUT ANYTHING BUT WRESTLING?? I'M GOING TO BED!!

SHEESH!

NAMES MAKING NEWS

Bill Apter Reporting

14

15

HOW WOULD YOU FEEL ABOUT TRAVELING TO MEMPHIS?
WRESTLER

OF COURSE! I TAKE THE SHOW ON THE ROAD ALL THE TIME.

THEY HAVE SHOWS EVERY WEEK AND THEY GOTTA PACK THE PLACE. BUT IT'S NOT LIKE NEW YORK. IT'S A MUCH SMALLER CITY.
THEY'RE MUCH MORE "CREATIVE" IN THEIR BOOKING.
WRESTLER

I'LL JUST CALL MY FRIEND JERRY "THE KING" LAWLER!

IT'S PAST MIDNIGHT IN MEMPHIS. IS HE EVEN GONNA ANSWER??

WRESTLING IS A LATE-NIGHT BUSINESS, PLUS ANY PROMOTER WILL GET UP OUT OF BED FOR A BUSINESS CALL.
RING!

RING!
THIS BETTER BE GOOD.

YOU'RE TELLING ME YOU GOT ANDY KAUFMAN IN YOUR ROACH-INFESTED APARTMENT??

OK, ANDY, HERE'S WHAT THE PLAN IS...

"FLY DOWN TO MEMPHIS AND WE CAN DO A FEW SHOWS AND FILM SOME STUFF BEFORE YOU HAVE TO GET BACK FOR 'TAXI.'"
YEAH, WE HAVE A MONTH OF SHOOTING AFTER THAT.

"WE'LL HAVE YOU CHANGE IN THE HEEL LOCKER ROOM."

LOOK AT THIS ASSHOLE. THINKS HE'S A WRESTLER.

SOME OF THESE WOMEN DOWN HERE IN MEMPHIS ARE PRETTY TOUGH. WHAT IF YOU LOSE?
HEAD OF THE PROMOTION

I'D PAY 'EM THE $500, BUT...
I REALLY DON'T THINK IT'S POSSIBLE.
I CAN BEAT ANY WOMAN.

I'M FROM NEW YORK CITY! AND I'VE TAKEN OVER HOLLYWOOD!!

SIMPLY BEING FROM NEW YORK MIGHT'VE BEEN ENOUGH TO HEAT UP THE CROWD.

BOOOO

I'VE BEATEN WOMEN FROM NEW YORK AND L.A.! MEMPHIS IS NOTHING!

WOMEN ARE SUITED BETTER FOR SCRUBBING THE POTATOES AND WASHING THE CARROTS!

I'VE GOT THE BRAINS!

NOW HE WAS INSULTING ALL OF MEMPHIS. THEY WANTED BLOOD!

THE FOURTH CHALLENGER WAS ABOUT TO REMIND ANDY WHY THEY STOPPED DOING OPEN CHALLENGES IN PRO WRESTLING YEARS AGO.

SHE OUTWEIGHED ANDY BY MORE THAN FIFTY LBS.

SHE WAS AN INSTANT HERO WITH FANS.

THESE WERE REAL AMATEUR WRESTLING MATCHES, BUT ANDY HAD SOME UNFAIR ADVANTAGES.

YES!

KILL HIM

THE WOMEN ALWAYS HAD TO PIN HIM. HE JUST HAD TO SURVIVE THREE MINUTES.

THE FACT FOXY DAMN NEAR KILLED HIM, NOT TO MENTION ALMOST PINNED HIM, DID NOT GO UNNOTICED BY JERRY LAWLER.

ANDY WAS A SKILLED PERFORMER, BUT THE ACT NEEDED TWEAKING.
JERRY "THE KING" KNEW HOW TO MAKE THIS INTO THE TRUE ART OF PRO WRESTLING.
JEEZ, MAN. THAT WAS SOME SERIOUS HEAT!

YOUR PROMOS GET THE FANS FIRED UP IN A BIG WAY.
RED HOT!!
EXACTLY WHAT YOU WANT. BUT...

OK, SO. THE FANS HATE YOUR ASS.

THANK YOU, MR. LAWLER.

YOU MAY NOT HAVE NOTICED THIS BUT...

WHEN FOXY SLAMMED YOU THE CROWD JUST WENT WILD.

THAT'S HOW WE SELL TICKETS.

YOU NEED A COMEUPPANCE.
OK, MR. LAWLER.
gulp.

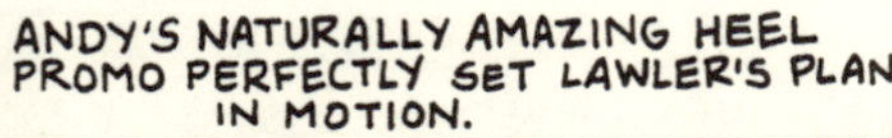
ANDY'S NATURALLY AMAZING HEEL PROMO PERFECTLY SET LAWLER'S PLAN IN MOTION.

LANCE, I'M NOT SAYING WOMEN AREN'T INTELLIGENT. THEY ARE! FOR SURE!
WHEN IT COMES TO THE COOKING AND CLEANING AND THE SCRUBBING THE POTATOES, WASHING THE CARROTS...
ANYTHING ELSE, THEY'RE ALL OATMEAL NORTH OF THE EYEBROWS! WHEATENA FOR BRAINS.

ON MONDAY THEY BROUGHT ANDY OUT AT THE LIVE SHOW BUT NOT TO WRESTLE. JUST PROMOTE. THEY HATED HIM SO MUCH.
HE WAS IN HEAVEN.
BOOO
UP YOURS
SCREW YOU

I'VE GOTTA GO BACK TO HOLLYWOOD...
...BUT I'LL BE BACK IN ONE MONTH.
THIS TIME I'LL OFFER $1,000!
AND MARRY THE GIRL!!

THE PLAN WAS TO GET AN ANGLE GOING BETWEEN ANDY AND JERRY.

BOO

THEY WING IT IMPROV-STYLE, WHICH WAS TOTALLY COMMON IN THIS ERA OF PRO WRESTLING.

I'M FROM HOLLYWOOD!!

SCRIPTING HURT THE REALISM OF THE EVENT.

GO FOXY!!

KICK HIS BUTT!

KAUFMAN, YOU THINK YOU'RE TOUGH?? GIVE HER THREE MORE MINUTES AND I BET SHE'LL WHIP YOU! DO IT, YOU COWARD! YELLOW BELLY!!

WHAT!!?

YOUR WINNER: ANDY KAUFMAN!

FINALLY, LAWLER PICKED HIS MOMENT.

FOXY ROLLED OUT OF THE RING AND ANDY FLIPPED OUT!
LAWLER, YOU DUMB APE!!
YOU DON'T TOUCH ME!
HE RECOGNIZED JERRY'S CUE AND STARTED GOADING HIM.

OOOH OOH-AHH AHH

SHOVE!!

THE CROWD WENT ABSOLUTELY BANANAS FINALLY SEEING ANDY GET A TINY BIT OF WHAT WAS COMING TO HIM.'

THIS WAS WHY THEY CAME: TO SEE GOOD TRIUMPH OVER EVIL.

ANDY WANTED TO BE A FULL-TIME WRESTLER, BUT HE ACTUALLY DID HAVE A HOLLYWOOD CAREER TO MAINTAIN.

HE MADE A FILM CALLED "HEARTBEEPS."

HE COSTARRED WITH BERNADETTE PETERS. BOTH PLAYED ROBOTS.

SORT OF A A ROMANTIC COMEDY "STAR WARS."

SISKEL & EBERT GAVE IT TWO THUMBS DOWN.

ROGER EBERT SAID OF THE FILM:

IT SUFFERS FROM TERMINAL CUTENESS.

Shapiro
Los Angeles
90210
DAVID LETTERMAN
P.O. BOX 771
NEW YORK, NY
12111

12:00
03
I'M FROM HOLLYWOOD!

HEH!
HAW!

I WILL SUE YOU!!

I NEED THIS ON MY SHOW!

THIS IS JUST ONE OF MY MANY MATCHES.
AND THIS IS IN MEMPHIS??

ANDY'S GRANDMA PEARL DIED SUDDENLY, AND HE DECIDED HE NEEDED TO VISIT HIS SURVIVING GRANDMA, GRANDMA LILLIE.

SHE LIVED IN HOLLYWOOD BY HERSELF.
HOLLYWOOD, FLORIDA

ON THE WAY TO HER PLACE, HE STOPPED TO GET HER A GIFT.

COLOR
BIG SCREEN
SORNY

SEARS

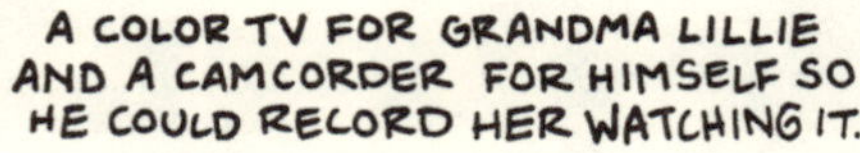
A COLOR TV FOR GRANDMA LILLIE AND A CAMCORDER FOR HIMSELF SO HE COULD RECORD HER WATCHING IT.

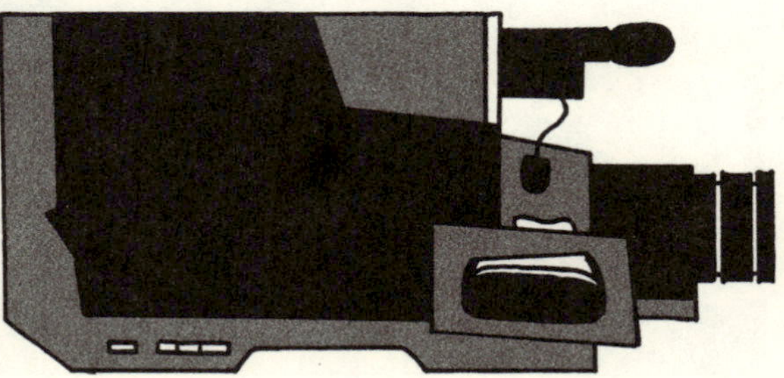

DO YOU WATCH ME ON "SATURDAY NIGHT LIVE," GRANDMA?
● RECORD
SOMETIMES.

AND YOU LIKE THE SHOW, RIGHT?
NO.

YOU ONLY WATCH TO SEE ME?
YES.

WHAT ABOUT WHEN I WRESTLE?
AUNT ESTHER
IT'S TERRIBLE!

I NEVER SAW HIM WRESTLE.
OH! YOU NEVER SAW HIM WRESTLE?
YOU DIDN'T MISS ANYTHING.

NEXT STOP ON HIS BREAK WAS THE MUSTANG RANCH IN NEVADA, A LEGAL HOUSE OF PROSTITUTION.

MUSTANG RANCH

*GEORGE SHAPIRO, ANDY'S MANAGER

I WAS THINKING: WHAT IF WE SET UP A NEW ORGANIZATION CALLED...

"MEN FOR THE PROMOTION OF WOMEN'S EQUAL RIGHTS."

THEN PEOPLE WILL KNOW HOW I TRULY FEEL EVEN THOUGH I WRESTLE WOMEN.

ANDY, JUST QUIT WRESTLING! IT'S TOO EXTREME!
PEOPLE ARE ACTUALLY STARTING TO HATE YOU! IT'S JUST DESTRUCTIVE TO YOUR CAREER.

I CAN STILL BE INNOCENT, THOUGH, RIGHT, GEORGE?

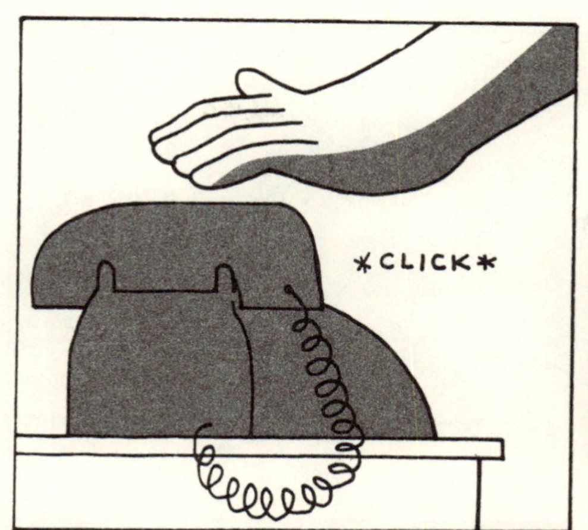
CLICK

OH! I SHOULD CALL HOME.

HI, ANDY! ARE YOU STILL AT CAMP?

HA-HA!
YES, MOM!

LATER:
I GUESS I AM AN EXTREMIST.

FORMER PRODUCER OF "SNL" DICK EBERSOL GOT ANDY TO HOST HIS NEW MUSIC SHOW: "MIDNIGHT SPECIAL."
I TRUSTED YOU!
I TRUSTED YOU!

ONE SEGMENT FEATURED AN ORIGINAL SONG CALLED:
I TRUSTED YOU!
I TRUSTED YOU!
I TRUSTED YOU!

I TRUSTED YOU!
I TRUST-ED YOU!

I TRUSTED YOU!!

I TRUSTED YOU!

I TRUSTED YOU!

I TRUSTED YOU!

BASSLINE

I TRUSTED YOU!

THE CROWD WAS RELIEVED. BUT THEN HOST WOLFMAN JACK SAID:
COME ON BACK OUT!!

I TRUSTED YOU!!
I TRUSTED YOU!!
NOW THE CROWD LOVED IT!!

I TRUSTED YOU!
I TRUSTED YOU!!

THERE WAS ALSO A TAPED SEGMENT OF ANDY'S WRESTLING EXPLOITS. HE EXPOSES ACTUAL WRESTLING BUSINESS SECRETS.

WHEN I DO THE WRESTLING ACT, I'M PLAYING A VILLAIN.
JUST LIKE ANY ACTOR.

"I'M TRYING TO GET PEOPLE TO DISLIKE ME... JUST LIKE THE BAD GUY IN ANY FILM."

"JUST SO THEY'LL GET REALLY EXCITED AND REALLY HATE ME AND REALLY ROOT FOR HER."

"WHEN I PLAY A ROLE WHETHER LOVED OR HATED, I PLAY IT TO THE HILT."

I GO ALL THE WAY.
NEVER BREAKING.

SOMEHOW ANDY'S REAL REVELATIONS ABOUT WRESTLING FLEW UNDER THE RADAR. THE "MIDNIGHT SPECIAL" AUDIENCE DIDN'T BELIEVE A WORD ANDY WAS SAYING, EVEN WHEN HE WAS TELLING THE TRUTH.

BUT HE WAS SERIOUS.

AND HIS WRESTLING PERSONA WAS NOW FULLY FORMED.

MEANWHILE, ON THE SET OF "TAXI."

DAMMIT!! WHERE IS KAUFMAN!?

HE'S STILL MEDITATING.

HE'S NEVER MEDITATING WHEN HE'S GOT A DAMN WRESTLING MATCH!!

MR. LAWLER, I'M READY TO COME BACK TO MEMPHIS TO WRESTLE!

OH MAN! DAMN! LISTEN, ANDY, HOW ABOUT YOU SEND US A TAPE? YOU'VE GOT A CAMERA, RIGHT? MAKE A TAPE FOR US.

WE'LL SET THE WHOLE THING UP PLAYING BITS AND PIECES ON OUR TV. WHEN YOU COME DOWN HERE, THE CROWD WILL BE RED HOT! WE'LL DO A WEEK-BY-WEEK BUILD.

I'M KIND OF NERVOUS ABOUT OUR MATCH. I DON'T WANNA GET HURT.

TRUST ME. IT'S AS SAFE AS CAN BE.

JERRY SET THE STAGE ON MEMPHIS TV. CHANNEL FIVE.

YOU ALL REMEMBER WHEN ANDY KAUFMAN FROM "TAXI" CAME DOWN HERE AND I HAD TO GET PHYSICAL WITH HIM?

WELL, YESTERDAY SOMEONE SHOWS UP AT MY DOOR...

THEY SHOT THE VIDEO IN GEORGE SHAPIRO'S BACKYARD.
TELL ME BEFORE YOU START.

DON'T MOVE. STAY IN FRAME.

ZMUDA PLAYED ANDY'S LAWYER.
...THEN I'LL GO...

REC

ANDY CUTS A WRESTLING PROMO ON JERRY LAWLER.

REMEMBER ME!?

ONLY A HANDFUL OF PERFORMERS IN THE HISTORY OF THE ART FORM WERE THIS GOOD. HE WAS A TOTAL NATURAL.

MR. LAWLER, I AM FROM HOLLYWOOD AND I HAVE A LOT OF MONEY.

I'VE GOT A HIGH-POWERED LAWYER, AND I WILL SUE YOU FOR EVERY PENNY!!

YOU WILL BE IN DEBT TO ME FOR THE REST OF YOUR LIFE!!

YOU'LL NEVER EAT AGAIN WHEN I'M THROUGH WITH YOU!!

JUST IN CASE YOU DON'T BELIEVE ME, I'VE BROUGHT MY LAWYER, MR. BOB ZMUDA.

ASSAULT AND BATTERY IS ASSAULT AND BATTERY.

IT DOESN'T MATTER IF IT'S ON THE STREETS OR IN THE RING.

YOU DIDN'T SIGN A CONTRACT TO FIGHT THIS MAN.

IT'S THE SAME AS A SPECTATOR JUMPING IN.

DO I HAVE A CASE?

YOU HAVE A PERFECT CASE.

WILL JERRY LAWLER EVER EAT AGAIN?

ONLY IF SOMEONE GIVES HIM A HANDOUT.

YOU SEE, I'VE GOT THE BRAINS!!

I'M FROM HOLLYWOOD.

I'M NOT A DUMB HICK FROM...

THIS RIDICULOUSLY EXAGGERATED STEREOTYPE SOUTHERN AFFECT WAS A VICIOUS ATTACK ON THE PEOPLE OF MEMPHIS.
MEMMM-PHISS

TENNNN-ESS-SEE.

LET ME TELL YOU WHAT I'VE FIGURED OUT ABOUT THIS ANDY KAUFMAN.
WHEN ANDY WAS A KID, HE FANTASIZED ABOUT BEING A WRESTLER.

UNFORTUNATELY WHEN HE GREW UP HE WAS A SKINNY IDIOT! A WIMP!!

HE KNEW HE COULD NEVER BE A WRESTLER.

SO HE HAD TO SETTLE ON BEING AN ACTOR AND A MOVIE STAR.

FINALLY, HE MAKES SO MUCH MONEY AND GETS SO FAMOUS...

HE THINKS TO HIMSELF:
NOW I CAN LIVE OUT MY FANTASY.

HE FIGURES THERE'S NO WAY HE CAN BEAT A MAN, SO HE WRESTLES WOMEN!
AND THEY DO IT! JUST TO GET A PIECE OF ANDY'S FAME.

AND HE GETS TO LIVE OUT HIS FANTASY!

LAWLER HAD HIM PEGGED.
HA HA

IF YOU REALLY WANNA LIVE OUT YOUR FANTASY, WE'LL DO IT MY WAY.
GET IN THE RING WITH ME AND I WILL END YOUR FANTASY.

OR WE CAN SETTLE IT IN COURT...
YOUR WAY.

YOU'RE A JOKE!!

THE AUDIENCE IS GONNA THINK THIS IS A WEEK LATER.
YOU JUST GOT CHALLENGED TO A MATCH.

DER!!
YOU WANNA RASSLE ME? MEMPHIS-STYLE??
FINE!

I'M NOT SCARED! I'VE WRESTLED WOMEN BIGGER THAN YOU!
AND SMARTER THAN YOU!
'CAUSE YOU'RE FROM MEMPHIS, TENNESSEE!

DUH!
DER

DUH!
DUH!

THIS WOMAN IS A LOT BIGGER THAN YOU, LAWLER!

THAT'S ENOUGH!!

LOOK, KAUFMAN, THIS IS MY JOB AND I TAKE IT SERIOUSLY! AND I DON'T LIKE PEOPLE COMIN' IN AND MAKIN' A JOKE OF IT!

AT THE MID-SOUTH COLISEUM YOU'RE GONNA GET HURT, SON.

LAWLER WAS THE VOICE OF THE PEOPLE.

AND THE PEOPLE WANTED BLOOD.

SELLOUTS WERE COMMON FOR THE MID-SOUTH COLISEUM.

AND LAWLER VS. KAUFMAN HAD A HOT SELLOUT CROWD.

THIS WAS THE REAL DEAL.

THE KING WAS ALSO ESCORTED BY POLICE.

BECAUSE EVERYONE JUST WANTED TO TOUCH A PIECE OF HIS GREATNESS.
I ♡ U.

THE KING WAS ABSOLUTELY BELOVED.

SINCE THE MATCH WOULD BE SHORT, THEY STALLED FOR A FEW MINUTES.
A CAT-AND-MOUSE GAME.

BOO

OOOH OOH
AHH AHH

GET BACK!

IDIOT!

LET'S GO!
COME ON, WIMP!!
QUIT RUNNIN'!

YOU DUMB APE!!
ZIP!

DID YOU COME HERE TO WRESTLE OR TO ACT LIKE AN ASS!?

JUST LIKE THEY'D PRACTICED THE DAY BEFORE IN THE PROMOTER JERRY CALHOUN'S BASEMENT...
BOO

THE KING OFFERED ANDY A HEADLOCK.

THEN I LIFT YOU UP AND WE BOTH GO DOWN TOGETHER, BOTH ABSORBING THE BLOW.

KILL HIM!

THEN LAWLER GOES FOR THE ILLEGAL PILEDRIVER MOVE.

THIS COULD HURT A LOT OR NOT AT ALL, DEPENDS ON HEAD PLACEMENT.

YOUR HEAD WONT HIT THE GROUND. JUST MY LEGS AND ASS.

"THEN SELL IT LIKE I JUST KILLED YOU."

THE REFEREE CALLED THE MATCH. LAWLER WAS DISQUALIFED.
DING DING!

THE CROWD LOST IT!!

GET HIM!

FINALLY SHUT HIM UP!

THE REF CHECKS ON ANDY, WHO IS FINE.

CAN YOU MOVE?

I'M OK. BUT I WANT AN AMBULANCE.

ANDY WANTS AN AMBULANCE.
WHAT!? HE'S FINE!
HE STILL WANTS ONE.

WE DON'T HAVE A KAYFABE AMBULANCE SET UP!

A REAL ONE WILL COST $3,000! TELL HIM NO.

CAN YOU BELIEVE THIS GUY??
HE'S NUTS.

HE SAYS HE'LL PAY FOR IT.
ALL RIGHT, FINE.

HERE COMES A REAL CITY AMBULANCE THAT COULD'VE BEEN DOING REAL WORK.
WEEE
WOOO
THE AMBULANCE TOOK ABOUT FIFTEEN MINUTES TO GET THERE. DANNY DAVIS FED LAWLER A LINE TO KEEP THE CROWD HOT.
HAW!
HEY! DON'T CALL HIM AN AMBULANCE, CALL HIM A TAXI!

THE COPS HAD TO DEFEND ANDY'S SEEMINGLY PARALYZED BODY WHILE THEY STRETCHERED HIM OUT.
THE CROWD STILL WANTED BLOOD.
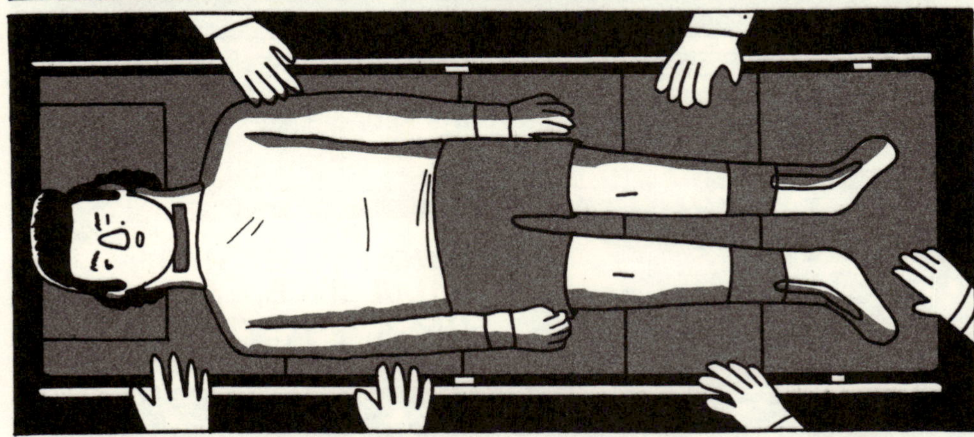

JUST LIKE BUDDY ROGERS.

ANDY SPENT THE NIGHT IN THE HOSPITAL.

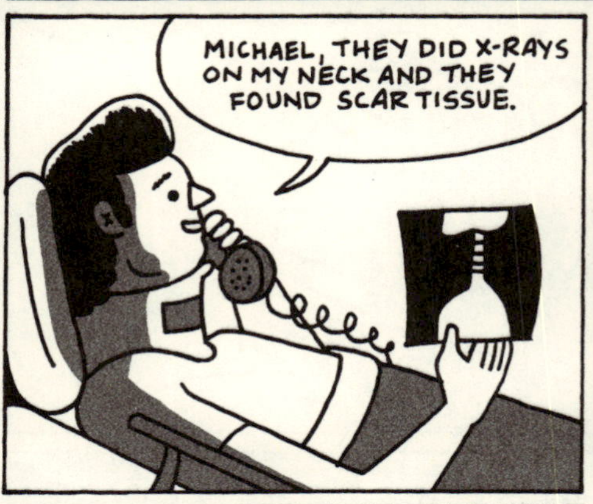
MICHAEL, THEY DID X-RAYS ON MY NECK AND THEY FOUND SCAR TISSUE.

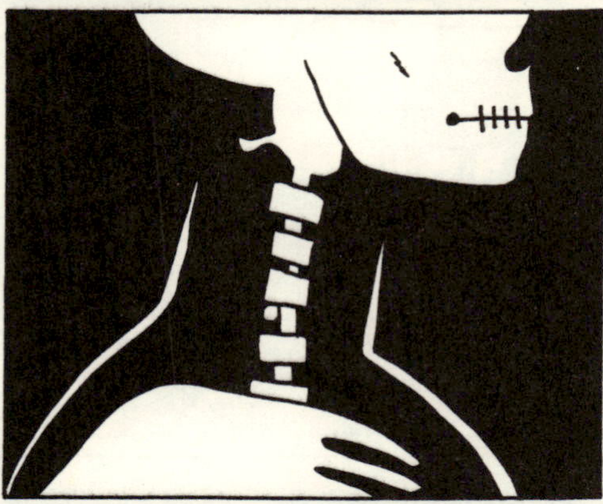

IT'S GOTTA BE FROM WHEN YOU SUPLEXED ME ON THE COUCH. REMEMBER?!

YES, ANDY.

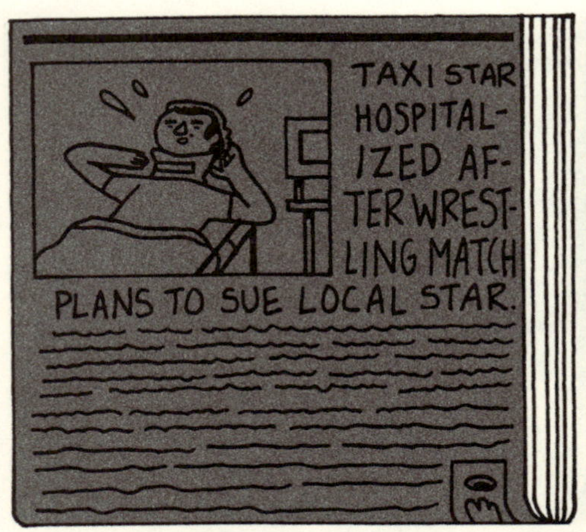
TAXI STAR HOSPITAL-IZED AF-TER WRESTLING MATCH
PLANS TO SUE LOCAL STAR.

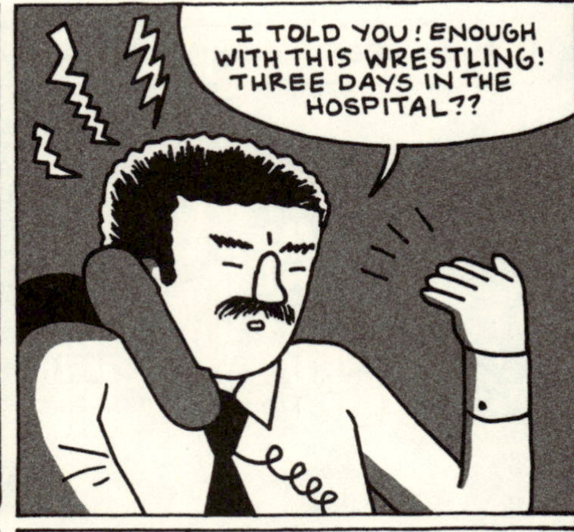
I TOLD YOU! ENOUGH WITH THIS WRESTLING! THREE DAYS IN THE HOSPITAL??

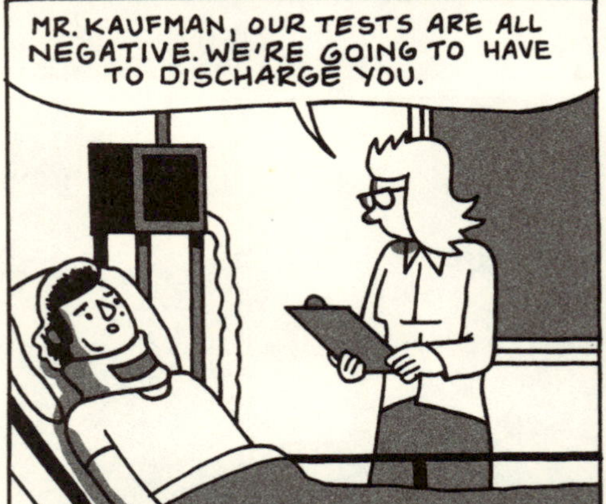
MR. KAUFMAN, OUR TESTS ARE ALL NEGATIVE. WE'RE GOING TO HAVE TO DISCHARGE YOU.

BUT MY NECK STILL HURTS.

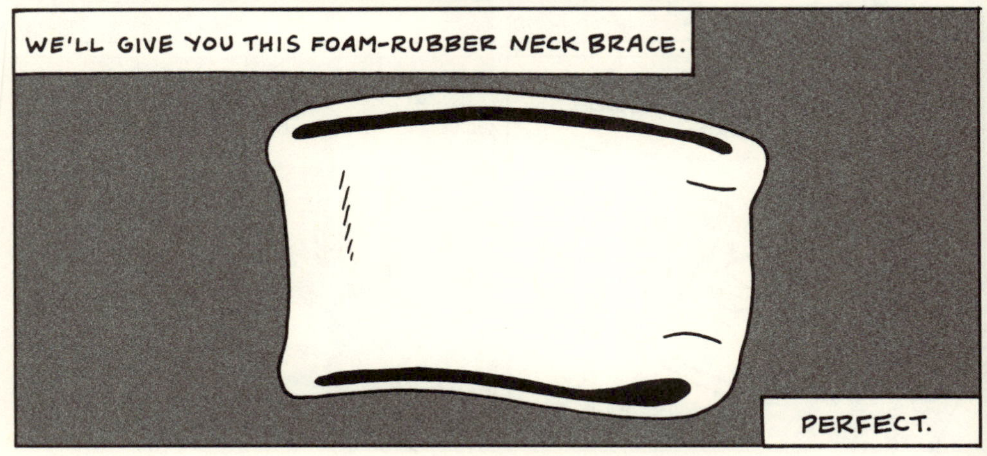
WE'LL GIVE YOU THIS FOAM-RUBBER NECK BRACE.
PERFECT.

LAWLER RECEIVED A THANK-YOU LETTER FOR PILEDRIVING ANI

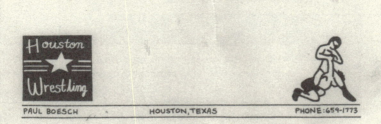

PAUL BOESCH HOUSTON, TEXAS PHONE: 659-1773

Dear Mr. Lawler,

I want to personally thank you for sticking up for the business against Andy Kaufman. Thanks for putting that punk Hollywood actor in his place and showing him what wrestling is all about.

Sincerely,

Paul Boesch

Paul Boesch,

President of Houston Wrestling

ANDY WORE THE NECK BRACE IN PUBLIC AT ALL TIMES FOR FIVE MONTHS.

THE PEOPLE OF MEMPHIS CERTAINLY BOUGHT IT.

BUT ANDY HAD A PLAN THAT WOULD HAVE THE WHOLE COUNTRY BUYING INTO IT.

HEY! LATKA!!

JERRY, DID GEORGE CALL YOU ABOUT LETTERMAN? TELL YOU WHAT THE PLAN IS?
YEAH...

YOU APOLOGIZE FOR MAKING FUN OF WRESTLING. THEN I'LL APOLOGIZE FOR HURTING YOU.

THEN I'LL SING, "WHAT THE WORLD NEEDS NOW IS LOVE. SWEET LOVE."

WHAT DO YOU THINK?
YEAH...
EH, IT'S OK.

WOULDN'T IT BE GREAT IF YOU JUST SLUGGED ME?

WELL, THEY PROBABLY WOULDN'T SHOW IT! AND THEN I'D GET ARRESTED.

YEAH, YOU'RE PROBABLY RIGHT.

LAWLER CAME TO NEW YORK CITY FOR DAVID LETTERMAN.
HE'D ARRANGED A PHOTO SHOOT WITH BILL APTER AND CRAIG PETERS FROM "PRO WRESTLING ILLUSTRATED."

I GOT YOU GUYS FULL ACCESS BACKSTAGE TONIGHT. THIS IS HUGE FOR WRESTLING.

MR. LAWLER, LET'S GO OVER THE SHOW ONE MORE TIME. SEGMENT ONE: WE SHOW CLIPS AND YOU GUYS ARGUE.
KNOCK
KNOCK
KNOCK

THEN WE GO TO A COMMERCIAL.
THEN ANDY SINGS...

DAMN, BILL, TWO SEGMENTS! THAT'S LIKE TWENTY MINUTES.

COME ON, YOU'RE A BIG TV STAR!

YEAH, ON MEMPHIS LOCAL TV.
THIS IS MILLIONS OF PEOPLE!

LAWLER KNEW ANDY WAS GONNA THROW AWAY THE SCRIPT IMMEDIATELY.

HE JUST HAD TO STAY TRUE TO THE KING PERSONA NO MATTER WHAT ANDY THREW AT HIM.

WRESTLING IS IMPROV, AND THIS WAS IS NO DIFFERENT FROM MONDAYS AT THE COLISEUM.

OK. FIRST IMPROVISATION: JERRY "THE KING" LAWLER WAS THE HEEL IN NEW YORK.

BOOOO

AS SOON AS HE SAT DOWN, BEFORE ANYONE SPOKE, SOMEONE IN THE CROWD YELLED:

HIT 'IM!

ANDY, DO YOU STILL NEED TO WEAR THE NECK BRACE? THE MATCH WAS IN APRIL, WASN'T IT?

ANDY IS DOING HIS CLASSIC BABE-IN-THE-WOODS INNOCENCE ROUTINE.
YES.

I'M NOT IN AS MUCH PAIN AS I ONCE WAS.
BUT IT STILL HURTS...

KIND OF A NAGGING INJURY, IS IT?

I DON'T KNOW WHAT IT'S CALLED, BUT I HAVE TO WEAR THE BRACE.
PSSH

HAHAHA HAW HAW

TO ME IT SEEMS LIKE YOU'D HAVE TO BE NUTS TO WANNA GET IN THE RING WITH THIS GUY...
HE'S TWICE YOUR SIZE...
HE'S BETTER LOOKING...
(APPLAUSE.)
JUST TEASING.
I WON SO MANY MATCHES WITH WOMEN I STARTED TO REALLY BELIEVE I WAS A GOOD WRESTLER.
ANDY WAS BEING TIMID BUT JOVIAL. HE WAS LULLING THE AUDIENCE INTO A FALSE SENSE OF SECURITY.
SHRUG

YOU SEE, I DON'T WANT TO SIT OUT HERE AND PRETEND LIKE WE'RE FRIENDS.
I THINK HE'S A WIMP.

I NOTICED PEOPLE BOOING ME AND I THINK YOU MIGHT'VE GOTTEN THE WRONG IMPRESSION. EVERYONE SEES ANDY AS HE IS NOW, THE LOVABLE LATKA.
BUT THAT'S NOT WHAT WE SAW IN MEMPHIS.

ANDY, YOU EGGED HIM ON.

IT WAS JUST TEASING! ALL IN FUN.

PFFT...

IT WAS JUST TEASING FOR FUN??
HA HA

LISTEN UP! I'M A BIG HOLLYWOOD STAR, OK?
YOU WANNA WRASSLE ME, MEMPHIS-STYLE!?
A-DER! DUH!
OK. WE'RE GONNA REGROUP HERE.
LET'S GO TO COMMERCIAL.
HOW COULD ANYONE BE MAD AT SOMETHING LIKE THAT? I WAS JUST KIDDING.

DAVE MADE SMALL TALK WITH JERRY.

HEY, DO YOU KNOW DICK THE BRUISER??

BACK FOR SEGMENT TWO...
I DON'T SEE HOW YOU CAN GET SO MAD FROM THAT. I WAS JUST PLAYING BAD-GUY WRESTLER! IT WAS JUST A ROLE. I WASN'T SERIOUS ABOUT IT. I DON'T TAKE THINGS LIKE THAT SERIOUSLY LIKE: "OH, I'M A STAR."

PSSH...

SO, YOU THINK HE OWES YOU AN APOLOGY, THEN?

ANDY WAS BLURRING REALITY. HE WANTED THE AUDIENCE TO TAKE HIM SERIOUSLY BEFORE. NOW HE WAS PLAYACTING.
YES. THAT'S WHY I CAME HERE. I'VE APOLOGIZED FOR ALL THE WRESTLING I'VE EVER DONE. ALL OF THE ABUSE I'VE GIVEN TO THE PEOPLE THAT DIDN'T UNDERSTAND WHAT I WAS DOING. AND I THINK AN APOLOGY TO ME IS SIMPLY IN ORDER. THAT'S ALL.

SO, IT'S COME TO THIS. YOU WANT JERRY TO APOLOGIZE?

NO, I DON'T THINK SO.

I DON'T THINK I OWE HIM AN APOLOGY. HE SAYS THIS IS ALL A BIG JOKE! WELL, I'M SURE IT WAS TO HIM...

DID YOU WANT TO HURT HIM?
WELL... YEAH.
I FELT I HAD TO.

IN ALL OF MY MATCHES-- AGAINST 400 WOMEN. I WAS BIGGER THAN MOST OF THEM--A LOT BIGGER! AND NEVER, NOT ONE TIME, DID ANYONE GET HURT.

YOU KNOW, IT'S SOMETHING I TAKE SERIOUSLY. IT'S HOW I MAKE MY LIVING--AND HE COMES MAKING A JOKE OF IT. HE'S HERE STILL WEARING, I DON'T KNOW IF IT'S A NECK BRACE OR FLEA COLLAR!

I HAD TO SPEND THREE DAYS IN THE HOSPITAL! IN TRACTION! I WAS GIVEN THIS NECK BRACE THERE!

BUT, ON THE OTHER HAND, NO ONE FORCED YOU TO GET IN THE RING, YOU KNOW?

THAT'S RIGHT. I DON'T COME OUT HERE AND TRY TO DO STAND-UP COMEDY. I'M A WRESTLER. YOU'RE A COMEDIAN...

IF YOU WERE THE MAN YOU SAY YOU ARE--YOU CALL YOURSELF A GREAT ATHLETE, A SPORTSMAN!
I NEVER SAID ANYTHING ABOUT BEING A SPORTSMAN.
NOW, LET ME...
LET ME...

WELL, I THOUGHT YOU WERE A PROFESSIONAL ATHLETE! YOU'RE ALWAYS TALKING ABOUT...

THAT'S RIGHT! I'M A PROFESSIONAL ATHLETE! YOU'RE A COMEDIAN! SO STAY OUT OF THE RING!
WELL, I WAS GOING TO THE RING. IT WAS SOMETHING I WAS DOING!

AS A JOKE, RIGHT?

IT'S NOT A JOKE TO ME.

DAVID LETTERMAN STRUGGLED BUT FINALLY REGAINED CONTROL OF THE INTERVIEW.

HE HAD TO RESPOND TO WHAT HE KNEW THE PEOPLE AT HOME WERE THINKING. THE GENERAL AUDIENCE WAS SKEPTICAL ABOUT WRESTLING AND ANDY KAUFMAN.

LET ME CLEAR UP ONE POINT HERE. THERE ARE A LOT OF PEOPLE WATCHING, THINKING WRESTLING IS A SHOW...

AND THIS MAY BE THE PINNACLE REPRESENTATION OF THAT. WAS THIS FIXED OR RIGGED?

ARE YOU TWO REALLY ENEMIES OR IS THIS A SCAM?

THIS WAS A LEGITIMATE QUESTION AT THE TIME. IT WAS THE QUESTION FOR PRO WRESTLING.

IF THIS WAS A FIGHT BREWING, PEOPLE WANTED IT TO BE REAL.

THE CROWD STARTED TO TURN ON ANDY AND GAIN SYMPATHY FOR JERRY. THEY BELIEVED THIS WAS LEGITIMATE.

SLAP!!

PRINCE

WHAT??

NO WAY.

JERRY KNEW "THE KING" WOULDN'T STAND FOR THAT SHIT.

BILL APTER'S CAMERA WAS JUST FLASHING AWAY.

HE KNEW THIS WAS A STORY BIGGER THAN THE WRESTLING WORLD.

BE RIGHT BACK!
LATE NIGHT WITH DAVID LETTERMAN
RING!!
HELLO? YEAH, I'M WATCHING!
YOU THINK THAT WAS REAL??

I AM SICK AND TIRED OF THIS
YOU ARE , MY FRIEND!
I WILL SUE YOUR !
WE'RE BACK AND—

YOU ARE A !

I'M SORRY TO USE THOSE WORDS, BUT YOU, SIR, ARE A !!

ANDY SUDDENLY TOSSED LETTERMAN'S COFFEE AT LAWLER.

THE KING CHASED ANDY OUT AND HE LEFT THE BUILDING!
ZIP!

LAWLER LEFT THE BACK WAY OUT.

WONDERING IF THEY'D EVEN AIR ANY OF IT.

BILL AND CRAIG BOLTED TO THE OFFICES OF THE "POST" TO DEVELOP THE FILM.

HOLD THAT ELEVATOR!

THEN THEY HEADED OVER TO LAWLER'S HOTEL ROOM.

ANDY ANSWERED THE DOOR.

HOW DID IT PLAY!?

SUBWAY HERO DIES SAVING PALS PAGES 3+4

WIN!!

EMPIRE POST

METRO

TODAY'S RACING

910,000

LATE NIGHT VIOLENCE

Comedian Kaufman's slap-fueled profanity-laced NBC tirade

SLAP-HAPPY PRO WRESTLER LAWLER

PRO WRESTLER JERRY "THE KING" LAWLER SLAPS COMEDIAN ANDY KAUFMAN ON "LATE NIGHT WITH DAVID LETTERMAN" ON NBC. KAUFMAN THEN USED SEVERAL PROFANITIES.

Firefighters released from hospital

PAGE THREE

JAILHOUSE LAWYER IN PATROL STORM

PAGE THIRTEEN

Mayor stuck in budget quagmire

PAGE TWO

M CORNETTE, WRESTLING PHOTOGRAPHER IN MEMPHIS TURNED WORLD FAMOUS MANAGER, ANNOUNCER, OWNER, PROMOTER, AND HISTORIAN
THIS DEAL BETWEEN LAWLER AND KAUFMAN WAS PROBABLY THE MOST BELIEVED THING IN WRESTLING OVER THE LAST FIFTY FUCKING YEARS!
ALL THESE PROMOTERS (INCLUDING VINCE MCMAHON, SR.) TURNED THEIR NOSES UP AT HAVING A CELEBRITY DO A MATCH BECAUSE NO ONE WOULD BUY IT!
AND LAWLER AND KAUFMAN MADE IT INTO A THING THAT GAVE WRESTLING THE MOST CREDIBILITY IT EVER GOT OVER THE LAST ERA.
ANDY COULD GET HEAT AND LAWLER WAS SUCH A SKILLED WRESTLER THAT HE COULD HAVE A BELIEVABLE MATCH WITH ANYONE OFF THE STREET.

NOT LONG AFTER THE LETTERMAN INCIDENT, DESPITE CRITICAL ACCLAIM, "TAXI" WAS CANCELED DUE TO SINKING RATINGS.

IT WAS REPLACED BY "NIGHT COURT."

ANDY CONTINUED PRO WRESTLING.

HE SLAPPED JERRY AROUND IN A HANDICAPPED MATCH. (TWO ON ONE)

HIS PARTNER WAS THE COLOSSUS OF DEATH, WHO WORE A RUBBER MASK.

AND HE GOT BEAT UP MORE THAN LAST TIME!

LISTEN, BABY, YOU CAME ASKIN' FOR MY HELP!! AND THEN YOU'RE COMING IN HERE AND TALKIN' ABOUT "I'M FROM HOLLYWOOD" AND I GOT A PLAN AND THAT...

JIMMY HART WAS A MUSICIAN AND ACTUAL POP STAR BEFORE BECOMING A COWARDLY HEEL MANAGER WHO <u>ALSO</u> HATED JERRY LAWLER.

HART WAS SAVED BY "BIG DADDY-O," A KNOCKOFF OF THE MORE WELL-KNOWN "SWEET DADDY SIKI."

AFTER THE BEATDOWN, ANDY WAS BACK ON MEMPHIS TV LOOKING FOR A CHAMPION.

FORGET THE MONEY. IF YOU QUIT, I'LL DO IT.

THIS ENDED UP JUST BEING A RUSE SET UP SO KAUFMAN AND HART COULD TURN ON LAWLER.

NOW THEY'RE PILE-DRIVING THE KING!!

WITH HELP FROM THE ASSASSINS AND HART, KAUFMAN DECLARED HIMSELF THE NEW KING OF WRESTLING.

HAHA HAHA!
THAT'S RIGHT, ALL YOU MEMPHIS HICKS!!

KAUFMAN...
IT TAKES MORE THAN THIS TO TAKE ME OUT.

THE FEUD COULD'VE GONE ON FOREVER.

ANDY HADN'T FORGOTTEN ABOUT "CLASSY" FREDDIE BLASSIE.

BLASSIE HAD RECORDED SOME SONGS BASED ON HIS CHARACTER AND BECOME A CULT HERO ON THE DR. DEMENTO RADIO SHOW.

HE WAS SEEN AS A CAMPY FIGURE, BUT HE DIDN'T QUITE PICK UP ON THE IRONY.

ANDY DID LOVE AND ADMIRE HIM AS A WRESTLER.

HE FIGURED EVERYONE JUST LOVED HIM BECAUSE HE WAS A FAMOUS CHAMPION WRESTLER.

BUT HE WAS ALSO AWARE OF HIS CAMP APPEAL.

SO WHEN ANDY CALLED FREDDIE ABOUT BEING IN A FILM WITH HIM, IT ONLY SEEMED NATURAL.
SAMMO'S
"MY BREAKFAST WITH BLASSIE" WAS AN AVANT-GARDE DOCUMENTARY-STYLE FILM WHERE THEY'D SIMPLY EAT AND TALK.
MOSTLY UNSCRIPTED, IT WAS ANDY AND HIS HERO AND EGGS.
I'VE GOT TO WASH MY HANDS.
I KEEP THESE WET WIPES WITH ME ALL THE TIME.
I WAS THE ONE THAT INTRODUCED THE FIRST BITING IN WRESTLING.
WOW.

I WANTED TO ASK YOU FOR ADVICE. SINCE MY INJURY, PEOPLE PUT ME DOWN FOR WRESTLING. WHAT CAN I DO?

WELL, LISTEN, PEOPLE THAT ARE DOWN IN THE MOUTH ABOUT IT...

TELL'EM: WELL, AT LEAST YOU TRIED!!

IT'S BETTER TO BE A HAS-BEEN THAN A NEVER-WAS.

YOU WERE IN THE MAIN EVENT IN ONE OF THE TOP CITIES IN THE SOUTH! YOU WERE RIGHT THERE. YOU WRESTLED IN FRONT OF A CAPACITY CROWD.

THE ONLY THING IS: DON'T ATTEMPT IT AGAIN.

I'VE SUFFERED NUMEROUS INJURIES IN MY PROFESSION.

SIX KNEE SURGERIES, SEVENTH AND EIGHTH VERTEBRAE FUSED TOGETHER, BROKE EVERY RIB ON THE RIGHT SIDE AND FIVE ON THE LEFT.

NECK BROKEN. FRACTURED SKULL. TWO CONCUSSIONS. NOSE BROKEN SEVEN TIMES. EVERY FINGER ON THE RIGHT SIDE...

I'VE BEEN CUT AND STABBED ELEVEN TIMES.
HAD ACID POURED ON ME.

BUT I'VE MET LOTS OF WONDERFUL PEOPLE. LOTS OF 'EM. ELVIS PRESLEY.

OH, ELVIS? HE WAS A FAN OF YOURS, WASN'T HE?

YES, I TOOK PUBLICITY PHOTOS WITH HIM. WHEN HE SAW ME HE SAID: "HELLO, FRED, HOW ARE YOU?"

AND HE WAS MUCH BETTER LOOKING IN PERSON. THE MOST HANDSOME MAN I'VE EVER SEEN.

THERE WAS A SCENE WHERE SOME GIRLS KEEP ASKING ANDY FOR HIS AUTOGRAPH. ONE WAS LYNNE MARGULIES, SISTER OF THE FILM'S DIRECTOR, JOHNNY LEGEND.
WHO ARE YOU?
HEY!
HI.

HEY, COME ON WE'RE TRYING TO EAT HERE.

THE SCENE WAS SET UP BUT ANDY ENDED UP DATING LYNNE SERIOUSLY.

THEY FELL IN LOVE.

LET ME INTRODUCE A MAN WHO IS A FIVE-TIME WORLD-WRESTLING CHAMPION, THE KING OF MEN, AND HOLLYWOOD FASHION PLATE OF WRESTLING: "CLASSY" FREDDIE BLASSIE!!

HE BROUGHT FRED ON "LETTERMAN."

SO WHAT DID YOU THINK OF ANDY'S WRESTLING?

WELL, I THINK HE SHOULD STICK TO WRESTLING WOMEN.
HE'S REALLY NOT QUALIFIED TO WRESTLE MEN.

AND THIS PHOTO? THIS IS YOU?

YES. I USED TO FILE DOWN MY TEETH AND BITE PEOPLE. THIS GUY GOT FORTY-EIGHT STITCHES.

WE'RE PLANNING ON REMAKING THE LAUREL AND HARDY FILM "SONS OF THE DESERT." WE'LL DO A LITTLE SCENE FOR YOU ALL.

THIS WAS SINCERE. BOTH REALLY WANTED TO DO THE FILM.

YOU'RE MANAGING ANDY NOW?

ONLY AS AN ENTERTAINER. NOT AS A WRESTLER. HE'S NOT A GOOD WRESTLER, BUT HE'S THE BEST ENTERTAINER.

HE'S A BETTER SINGER THAN PERRY COMO, BING CROSBY, ELVIS PRESLEY. AS A DANCER HE MAKES FRED ASTAIRE LOOK LIKE HE HAS TWO LEFT FEET.

I ONLY HANDLE THE BEST: BIG JOHN STUDD "CRIPPLER" STEVENS, IVAN KOLOFF, AND YOU!

GET OVER THERE AND SING! WHEN I SAY SING, YOU SING!
NOW!

HE SINGS A GOOFY GIBBERISH SONG AND DANCES LIKE AN IDIOT.

BLASSIE LOOKS ON IN DISGUST.
YEESH.

BACK IN MEMPHIS, LAWLER THREW A FIREBALL IN ANDY'S FACE!!

ANDY SENT IN MORE TAPES.
I WOULD LOVE TO WRESTLE YOU INSIDE A STEEL CAGE.
BUT YOU MADE ME SIGN A CONTRACT TO NEVER WRESTLE AGAIN!

SEE THIS, YOU MEMPHIS HICKS!!? THIS IS SOAP. S-O-A-P. YOU'VE PROBABLY NEVER HEARD OF IT. FIRST, YOU WET YOURSELF AND THEN RUB THIS ON YOUR BODY SO YOU WON'T STINK.

HE CALLED MEMPHIS TV.
IF I EVER GOT BACK IN THE RING, I WOULD KNOCK HIM OUT!! I WOULD KNOCK HIM OUT!!!

TELL LAWLER I'LL SEE HIM IN COURT!! I'LL SEE HIM IN COURT!!! AHH! AHH!! (SCREAMS UNINTELLIGIBLY)

BACK ON "LETTERMAN."
THERE ARE TWO PEOPLE IN MY LIFE I'VE NEVER TOLD I LOVE THEM, AND I'D LIKE TO BRING THEM OUT HERE NOW.
LADIES AND GENTLEMEN...
MY PARENTS.
AND THERE THEY WERE, STANLEY AND JANICE KAUFMAN ON "LATE NIGHT WITH DAVID LETTERMAN."
MOMMY AND DADDY, I LOVE YOU.
I'M SORRY FOR ALL OF THE PROBLEMS I GAVE YOU.

SO WHAT DO YOU THINK OF ANDY WRESTLING WOMEN?

OOOOH...
OH OH OH...

OH...
I HATE IT.

AND I STILL HAVEN'T SEEN THE TAPE OF HIM GETTING HURT. I CAN'T WATCH IT.

I LIKED WHEN HE DID ELVIS.

I WAS VERY ANGRY WITH JERRY LAWLER.
YES.

HE TOOK ADVANTAGE OF ANDY'S AMATEURISM.
AND HE DID REAL DAMAGE.

DIDN'T ANDY, Y'KNOW, KIND OF GOAD HIM INTO IT?

WELL, LOOK...
ANDY DID DO A LOT OF GOADING.

BUT THAT WAS AN ILLEGAL HOLD!!

CAN WE CALL MY GRANDMA?
YOU'VE GOT THE NUMBER?
HI, GRANDMA? IT'S ANDY. I WANTED TO SAY I LOVE YOU.
AND I LOVE YOU.
YOU'RE NOT WRESTLING ANYMORE, ARE YOU?

ONE NIGHT IN BED WITH HIS GIRLFRIEND, THANKSGIVING, 1983:

HE'D DEVELOPED LARGE-CELL CARCINOMA, CANCER OF THE LUNGS. IT HAD ALREADY SPREAD TO HIS THROAT. A TUMOR HAD CAUSED PNEUMONIA.

AFTER THE SHOW, HE TOLD JERRY ABOUT HIS DIAGNOSIS. HE WOULD NEVER RETURN TO MEMPHIS.

I'LL BE FINE.

SO SORRY.

JIMMY HART EVEN USED ANDY'S DIAGNOSIS IN AN ANGLE.

IN MAY 1984, ANDREW GEOFFREY KAUFMAN DIED OF CANCER.

HE WAS THIRTY-FIVE YEARS OLD.

LAWLER NEEDED TO ACKNOWLEDGE HIS DEATH ON TV BUT HAD TO STAY IN CHARACTER. ANDY WOULD UNDERSTAND.

I'M THE WRONG PERSON TO ASK ABOUT KAUFMAN. I HATED HIM AND HE HATED ME. I'M SORRY HE DIED, BUT...

THEY WERE FRIENDS.

I ALWAYS THOUGHT IF SOMEONE DIED YOU'D TALK TO SOMEONE WHO LIKED THEM! IF I DIE, DON'T TALK TO JIMMY HART!

NOW ON MONDAY NIGHT HUMONGOUS IS DEAD MEAT!!

AT ANDY'S REQUEST, "CLASSY" FREDDIE BLASSIE WAS RIGHT UP FRONT WITH THE KAUFMAN FAMILY.

IT WOULD'VE BEEN IMPOSSIBLE TO MAINTAIN THE GRUFF EXTERIOR OF THE "CLASSY" FREDDIE BLASSIE CHARACTER IN THE WAKE OF THE DEATH OF HIS REAL FRIEND.

MISSING FROM ATTENDANCE WAS THE CAST OF "TAXI."

WHEN ASKED ABOUT IT LATER, CAST MATE MARILU HENNER SAID:

WE ALL THOUGHT THIS WAS JUST ANOTHER ONE OF ANDY'S PUT-ONS. NONE OF US BELIEVED HIM.

MR.T! FROM TV'S "THE A-TEAM" AND "ROCKY III."

IN 1985, AFTER ANDY'S DEATH AND THE DEATH OF VINCE MCMAHON, SR., VINCE, JR., BROUGHT CELEBRITIES INTO HIS WWF WRESTLING ORGANIZATION AND ENTERED THE MAINSTRE

CYNDI LAUPER TOOK HULK HOGAN TO THE GRAMMYS.

AND THE HULKSTER APPEARED ON "SATURDAY NIGHT LIVE."

DICK EBERSOL AT NBC EVEN HELPED PRODUCE A LATE-NIGHT WRESTLING SHOW THAT RAN IN "SNL"'S TIME SLOT.

SATURDAY NIGHT'S MAIN EVENT

CELEBRITIES WOULD BECOME A MAINSTAY IN WRESTLING

RUMORS OF ANDY FAKING HIS DEATH BEGAN IMMEDIATELY AND CONTINUE TO THIS DAY.

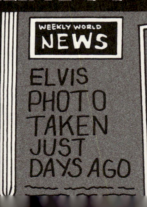

NOW APPEARING
NOW APPEARING
TONY CLIFTON
LIVE TONIGHT
NOW ON STAGE
OPEN FOR LUNCH
BRUNCH 10 AM

THE RUMORS ARE CERTAI FUELED BY BOB ZMUDA DOING THE TONY CLIFTON CHARACTER HIMSELF AFTE ANDY DIED.

PEOPLE DIDN'T BELIEVE IT BECAUSE THEY'D BEEN HAD BY ANDY SO MANY TIMES.

OR MAYBE IT'S BECAUSE HE IS TREASURED.

JUST LIKE ELVIS.

WEEKLY WORLD
NEWS
ELVIS PHOTO TAKEN JUST DAYS AGO

WHAT DO YOU THINK ABOUT THE ANDY-FAKED-HIS-DEATH THING?
MICHAEL KAUFMAN
BOX BROWN
WELL, IT WOULD BE NICE. BUT I WAS AT HIS FUNERAL. I SAW THE CASKET GO IN THE GROUND.
I HAVE ONE STORY I ALWAYS TELL ABOUT MY BROTHER.
THIS WAS WHAT ANDY WAS REALLY LIKE.

10 000
9 875
9 750
ARCADE
HEY, MICHAEL! CHECK OUT THIS GUY!
HEY YOU, KID! WHAT, THIS GAME HERE!?

I'M A WINNER, KID.
HEY WHAT'S THIS GAME HERE?
HOW DO YOU WIN?? TELL ME HOW TO WIN AND THEN I'LL WIN!!
HIT THIS THING?? FINE, WHAT DO I CARE!?
THIS AIN'T A PROBLEM FOR ME!
LEMME SEE HERE.
NO PROBLEM.
DROP!

HEY! IT'S THAT GUY FROM "TAXI"!!
BOY
OH, HEY! IT'S LATKA!
HEY!
HAHAHAHA!
HA! WHAT AN IDIOT!
BEACH
YOU HEAR ME!?
THIS IS HOW IT'S DONE.

AND BY THE TIME HE FINALLY QUIT...

OK, OK! ONE AT A TIME HERE!

IN 1999 A FILM WAS MADE ABOUT ANDY'S LIFE.

MY BROTHER JUST WASN'T LIKE THAT. HE WAS BRILLIANT AND KIND.

DO YOU KNOW THE SONG "THIS FRIENDLY WORLD" BY FABIAN? IT GOES SOMETHING LIKE: IN THIS FRIENDLY WORLD WHY SHOULD ANYONE BE AFRAID? WHY SHOULD ANYONE BE LONELY?—IT'S SOMETHING LIKE THAT... ANDY REALLY BELIEVED IN THAT. HE USED TO END HIS SHOWS SINGING IT. THAT'S HOW HE WANTED PEOPLE TO FEEL WHEN THEY LEFT.

AND I JUST WANNA SAY, UNTIL WE MEET AGAIN...
YUP. IT'S A FRIENDLY WORLD. AND WE SHOULD TREAT EACH OTHER LIKE SISTERS AND BROTHERS.

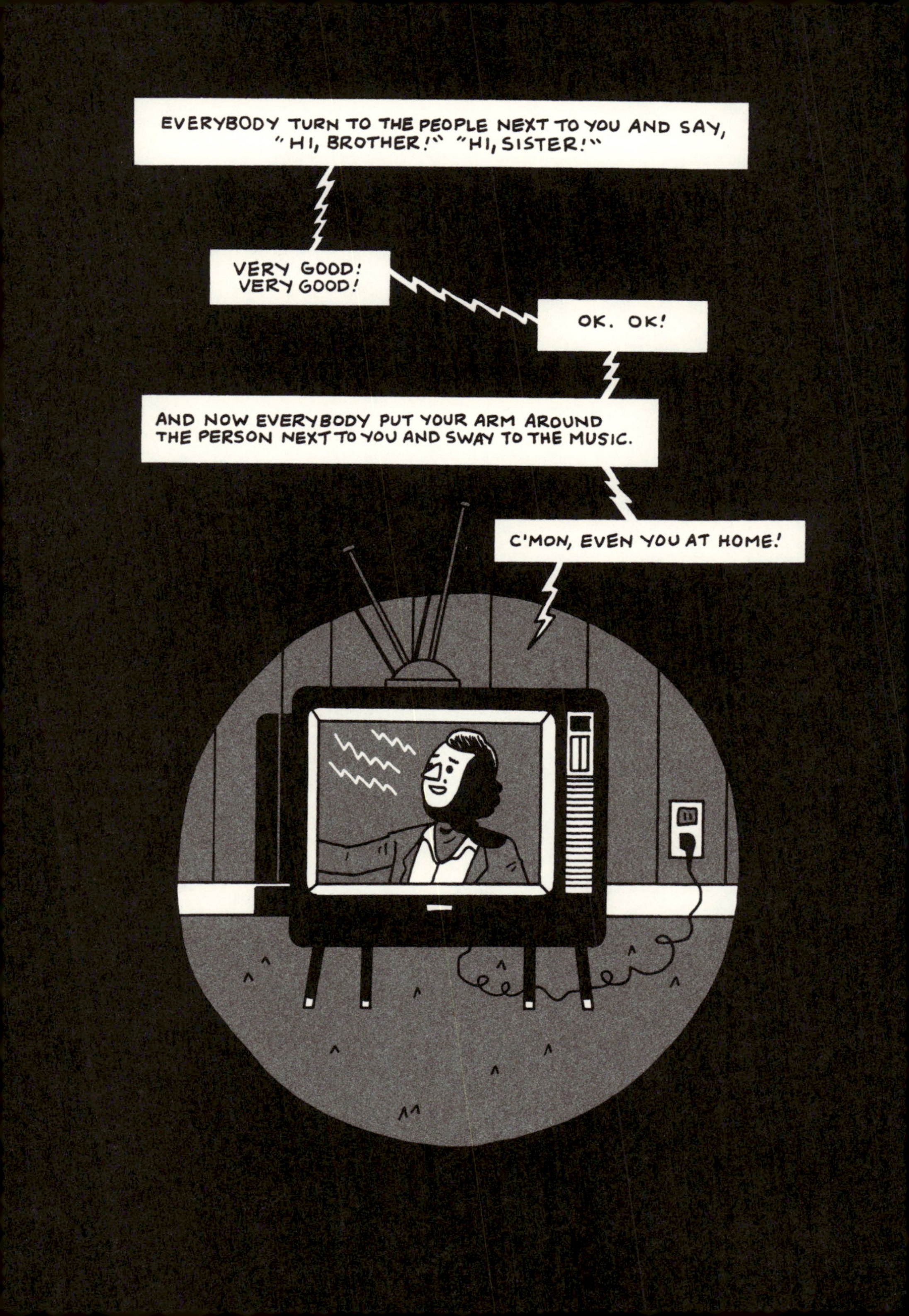

EVERYBODY TURN TO THE PEOPLE NEXT TO YOU AND SAY, "HI, BROTHER!" "HI, SISTER!"

VERY GOOD! VERY GOOD!

OK. OK!

AND NOW EVERYBODY PUT YOUR ARM AROUND THE PERSON NEXT TO YOU AND SWAY TO THE MUSIC.

C'MON, EVEN YOU AT HOME!

Bibliography

Apter, Bill. *Is Wrestling Fixed? I Didn't Know it was Broken: From Photo Shoots and Sensational Stories to the WWE Network, Bill Apter's Incredible Pro Wrestling Journey.* Toronto: ECW Press, 2015.

Apter, Bill. "Way Back Wednesday: John Tolos Talks Freddie Blassie, Victor Rivera, Bruno, & More..."*1 Wrestling* (blog). May 6, 2015. http://www.1wrestling.com/2015/05/06/way-back-wednesday-john-tolos-talks-fred-blassie-victor-rivera-bruno-more/.

African Drumming Techniques with Babatunde Olatunji. Interworld. Guilford, VT: *Andy's Funhouse* (TV Special). Written by Andy Kaufman and Mel Sherer. ABC. Interworld. August 28, 1979.

Andy Kaufman Plays Carnegie Hall. Written by Andy Kaufman and Bob Zmuda. Los Angeles, CA: Paramount, 1980.

The Andy Kaufman Show (TV Special). Directed by Dick Carter. PBS. July 15, 1983.

"*The Andy Kaufman Show: Blueprint for an Illusion.*" *Found in the Funhouse: The Disappearance of Andy Kaufman* (blog). June 24, 2009 (2:34 a.m.). http://foundinthefunhouse.blogspot.com/2009/06/andy-kaufman-show-blueprint-for.html.

Andy Kaufman: World Inter-Gender Wrestling Champion. England: Micro Werks, 2010. DVD.

Baucher, Brian. "Andy Kaufman, Artist?" *Art in America.* December 13, 2012. http://www.artinamericamagazine.com/news-features/news/andy-kaufman-maccarone/.

Blassie, "Classy" Freddie and Keith Elliot Greenberg. *The Legends of Wrestling—"Classy" Freddie Blassie: Listen, You Pencil Neck Geeks.* New York: Gallery Books, 2004.

Blassie, Freddie. *Nothin' but a Pencil Neck Geek.* Claremont, CA: Rhino Records, 1985. Record.

Bowden, Scott. "Simply Fabulous: WWE Hall of Famer Jerry Lawler Shares His Memories of Memphis Wrestling Legend Jackie Fargo." *Scott Bowden Presents Kentucky Fried Rasslin* (blog). June 24, 2013. http://kentuckyfriedwrestling.com/theword2/tag/jackie-fargo/.

"Bruno Sammartino Wins the World Championship Title!" *Chiller Theater Memories*. http://www.chillertheatermemories.com/SWMSammartino1.html.

"Andy Kaufman Wrestles Jim Hart." WSMV. July 16, 1983. Channel 4 News Report. "Tojo Yamamoto." WSMV. November 1992.

Classic Memphis Wrestling: 1981. "Memphis TV 3-14-81." Wrestling Epicenter Store. DVD.

Classic Memphis Wrestling: '70s Arena Matches. "Jackie Fargo vs. Jerry Lawler." Langhorne, PA: RF Video. DVD.

Classic Memphis Wrestling: '70s Arena Matches. "Jerry Lawler vs. Bobo Brazil." Langhorne, PA: RF Video. DVD.

Classic Memphis Wrestling: Jerry Lawler vs. Andy Kaufman. Langhorne, PA: RF Video. DVD.

Collins, Scott. "Jerry Lawler: Why His Andy Kaufman Wrestling Match Still Resonates." *The Los Angeles Times*. November 15, 2003. http://www.latimes.com/entertainment/tv/showtracker/la-et-st-jerry-lawler-why-his-andy-kaufman-wrestling-match-resonated-20131115-story.html.

Cornette, Jim, and Mark James. *Rags, Paper and Pins: The Merchandising of Memphis Wrestling*. Charleston, SC: CreateSpace Independent Publishing Platform, 2013.

Creahan, D. "AO on Site: New York—Opening of Andy Kaufman 'On Creating Reality' at Maccarone Gallery Through February 16, 2013." *Art Observed*. January 16, 2013. http://artobserved.com/2013/01/ao-on-site-new-york-opening-of-andy-kaufman-on-creating-reality-at-maccarone-gallery-through-february-162013/.

The Death of Andy Kaufman. Directed by Christopher Maloney. Written by Christopher Maloney. Wild Eye Releasing, 2011.

DeMain, Bill. "The Time Andy Kaufman Wrestled a Bunch of Women." *Mental Floss*. July 2, 2012. http://mentalfloss.com/article/31079/time-andy-kaufman-wrestled-bunch-women.

Desmon, Stephanie. "Skip the Grades, Just Play the Tape." *The Baltimore Sun*. May 23, 2001. http://articles.baltimoresun.com/2001-05-23/news/0105230212_1_andy-kaufman-peckham-english-teacher.

Drash, Wayne. "The Great Ruse: The Comedic Genius Who Rock Wrestling." *CNN*. April 7, 2012. http://www.cnn.com/2012/04/07/us/kaufman-lawler-wrestling-match/.

Ehret, Theo. "Fight Night at the Olympic: Class Los Angeles Ringside Photography." *Fightland.* Vice.com. June 16, 2014. http://fightland.vice.com/blog/fight-night-at-the-olympic-classic-los-angeles-ringside-photography.

Eisenberg, Eric. "Andy Kaufman May Really Be Alive, Suggests News Reports." *CinemaBlend.* 2014. http://www.cinemablend.com/new/Andy-Kaufman-May-Really-Alive-Suggests-Reports-40294.html.

Fabian. "This Friendly World." Sony Music, 1959.

Getlen, Larry. "Friend: Andy Kaufman is Still Alive." *New York Post.* September 28, 2014. http://nypost.com/2014/09/28/why-andy-kaufman-might-still-be-alive/.

"Heyman Hustle on Yahoo Sports: Why Andy Kaufman Would Have Loved Wrestlemania." *Yahoo! News.* March 30, 2016. https://www.yahoo.com/news/blogs/the-turnstile/heyman-hustle-on-yahoo-sports-why-andy-kaufman-would-have-loved-wrestlemania-000700735.html?ref=gs.

"Hubert's: Freaks and Fleas in Times Square." *Ephemeral New York* (blog). November 30, 2009 (12:37 a.m.), https://ephemeralnewyork.wordpress.com/2009/11/30/huberts-a-museum-of-freaks-in-times-square/.

I'm From Hollywood: Andy Kaufman's Hilarious Adventures in the World of Professional Wrestling! Directed by Lynne Margulies. Tokyo: Legend House, 2007. DVD.

"'I Was in the Room': Andy Kaufman's Former Girlfriend Says She Watched Comedian Die in Hollywood Hospital in 1984, Rubbishing 'Daughter's' Claims He Is Still Alive." *Daily Mail.* November 15, 2013. http://www.dailymail.co.uk/news/article-2507817/Andy-Kaufmans-girlfriend-says-watched-comedian-die-Hollywood-hospital-1984.html.

Jerry Lawler Shoot Interview. Langhorne, PA: RF Video, 2001. DVD.

Jim Barniak's Sports Scrapbook. "Interview with Buddy Rogers." Philadelphia, PA: Prism, 1981.

Keller, Florian. *Andy Kaufman: Wrestling With the American Dream.* Minneapolis: University of Minnesota Press, 2005.

Late Night with David Letterman. "Episode #1.11." NBC. February 17, 1982.

Late Night with David Letterman. NBC. November 17, 1982.

Lawler, Jerry. *It's Good to be the King…Sometimes.* New York: Gallery Books, 2001.

James, Mark. *Memphis Wrestling History Presents: 1982*. Charleston, SC: CreateSpace, 2010.

Jenson, Bill. "Waking Andy Kaufman." *The Village Voice*. November 9, 1999. http://www.villagevoice.com/long-island-voice/waking-andy-kaufman-7155574.

Kennedy at Night. WLS-TV Chicago. June 1972.

Margulies, Lynne (ed.), and Bob Zmuda. *Dear Andy Kaufman, I Hate Your Guts!* Los Angeles: Process, 2009.

Margulies, Lynne, and Bob Zmuda. *Andy Kaufman: The Truth, Finally*. Dallas, TX: Benbella Books, 2014.

Matheson, Danielle. "David Letterman, Andy Kaufman, and the Interview That Changed Pro Wrestling in Pop Culture." *Uproxx*. January 17, 2017. http://uproxx.com/prowrestling/david-letterman-andy-kaufman-and-the-interview-that-helped-change-pro-wrestling-in-popular-culture/.

McMillen, J.K. "Shifting the Spotlight: Andy Kaufman." *Cageside Seats*. January 1, 2016. http://www.cagesideseats.com/2016/1/1/10697990/shifting-the-spotlight-andy-kaufman.

Memphis Heat: The True Story of Memphis Wrasslin'. Directed by Chad Schaffler. 2011. Universal City, CA: Distribber, 2011. DVD.

Memphis Wrestling in the '70s: Volume 2. 70s-tv.com. DVD.

Mr. Blassie Goes to Washington. Directed by Jeff Krulik. 1994.

My Breakfast with Blassie. Directed by Linda Lautrec and Johnny Legend. Written by Linda Lautrec and Johnny Legend. Los Angeles: Artist Endeavours International, 1983.

The Midnight Special. "Episode #9.17." Directed by Tom Trbovich. NBC. January 23, 1981. Pierce, Tony. "Paul Shaffer Knows What to Spill—and Not—in His Memoir." *The Los Angeles Times*. November 9, 2009. http://latimesblogs.latimes.com/jacketcopy/2009/11/paul-shaffer-andy-kaufman-david-letterman-1.html.

Saturday Night Live. "Ted Knight/Desmond Child & Rouge." NBC. December 22, 1979.

Schieb, Philip, and Marshall Barer. "Mighty Mouse Theme." *Mighty Mouse*. CBS. 1955–1956.

Smith, Roberta. "A Comedian as Artist: 'Creating Reality, by Andy Kaufman' at Maccarone." *The New York Times*. February 8, 2013. http://www.nytimes.com/2013/02/09/arts/design/creating-reality-by-andy-kaufman-at- maccarone.html?_r=0.

Steinberg, Avi. "Is Andy Kaufman Alive?" *The New Yorker*. March 31, 2015. http://www.newyorker.com/culture/culture-desk/the-belief-that-andy- kaufman-is-alive.

Steve Dahl & Gerry Meier. "Guest Caller Andy Kaufman." WLS FM 95. Chicago, IL. February 21, 1983.

Tomorrow Coast to Coast with Tom Snyder. NBC. August 22, 1979.

Thomas, Bryan. "'My Breakfast with Blassie': Andy Kaufman Meets Outrageous Wrestling Legend Freddie Blassie in a Downtown L.A. Diner." *Night Flight Plus*. January 21, 2017. http://nightflight.com/my-breakfast-with-blassie-andy-kaufman-meets-outrageous-wrestling-legend-freddie-blassie-in-a-downtown-l-a-diner/.

Pittsburgh Wrestling. Civic Arena. Pittsburgh, PA. March 18, 1963.

WTF with Marc Maron (Podcast). "Bob Zmuda." Howl.fm. April 25, 2012.

WTF with Marc Maron (Podcast). "Budd Friedman." Howl.fm. November 28, 2012.

WWF Houseshow. Madison Square Garden. New York, NY. October 22, 1979.

WWF Houseshow. Madison Square Garden. New York, NY. May 17, 1963.

Zehme, Bill. *Lost in the Funhouse: The Life and Mind of Andy Kaufman*. New York: Delacorte Press, 1999.

Zmuda, Bob, and Matthew Scott Hansen. *Andy Kaufman Revealed!: Best Friend Tells All*. Boston: Little, Brown and Co., 1999.

Web Resources

"1962–1965." *Graceland: The Home of Elvis Presley*. Accessed January 22, 2017. https://www.graceland.com/elvis/biography/1962_1965.aspx.

"1974." *The History of the WWE*. Accessed January 22, 2017. http://www.thehistoryofwwe.com/74.html.

"Andy Kaufman." *Internet Movie Database*. Accessed January 22, 2017. http://www.imdb.com/name/nm0001412/.

"Andy Kaufman." *New York Public Library Digital Collection*. Accessed January 22, 2017. https://digitalcollections.nypl.org/search/index?utf8=%E2%9C%93&keywords=%22andy%2Bkaufman%22#.

"Andy Kaufman." *The Professional Wrestling Museum*. Accessed January 22, 2017. http://www.wrestlingmuseum.com/pages/wrestlers/andykaufman2.html.

"Andy Kaufman's Letter to Elvis Presley." *The Andy Kaufman Homepage*. Accessed January 22, 2017. http://andykaufman.jvlnet.com/elvisletter.html.

"Andy Kaufman: The Truth, Finally." *Andy Kaufman Returns*. Accessed January 22, 2017. http://www.andykaufmanreturns.com/.

"Elvis Presley 1957–1958." *Elvis Presley Music*. Accessed January 22, 2017. http://www.elvispresleymusic.com.au/articles/elvis-presley-1957-1958-bu.html.

"Tony Clifton." *Wally on the Web*. Accessed January 22, 2017. http://www.wallyontheweb.com/tonyclifton.php.

Personal Interviews

Bob Zmuda. Interview by Box Brown. December 7, 2016.

Keith Elliot Greenberg. Interview by Box Brown. December 8, 2016.

Mark James. Interview by Box Brown. April 16, 2016.

Michael Kaufman. Interview by Box Brown. March 15, 2016.

Special thanks go to Mark James,
Keith Elliot Greenberg, and Josh Bayer
for their unending generosity,
especially on the subject of Andy.

Thank you also to my supportive
family, friends, editors, readers, wrestling
fans, and most of all you.

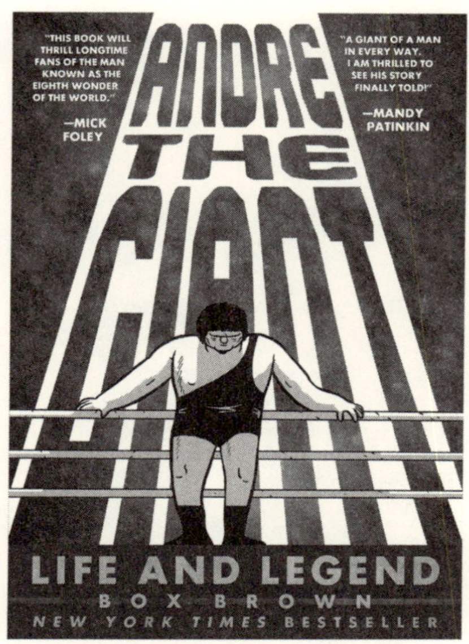

Andre the Giant: Life and Legend

"Its warts-and-more depiction of the French-born figure's odd life is ably illuminated by Brown in a stylized but engaging manner." —*Miami Herald*

"This comic is one that breaks the kayfabe—the wrestler's fourth wall—not just of the performer but of the man". —*National Post*

Tetris: The Games People Play

"The story never stops moving until its final pieces are in place." —*The New York Times*

"Against the backdrop of the Cold War, the saga of Tetris played out like a spy thriller—tragic deaths, corporate conspiracies, the prestige of nations hanging in the balance." —*Boston Globe*

"This is a work about the bittersweet dissonances of artistic creativity and commercial greed and the ephemeral yet crucial joy we get from making things fall into place." —*io9*

"*Tetris* is a remarkably spare work, cleanly and effortlessly introducing countless real-life characters and companies that intersect and tangle together in a game of tug-of-war." —*GQ*

"A rich read that provides valuable context for the rise of video games in the late twentieth century." —*A.V. Club*

Published by First Second

First Second is an imprint of Roaring Brook Press, a division of
Holtzbrinck Publishing Holdings Limited Partnership
175 Fifth Avenue, New York, New York 10010

Library of Congress Control Number: 2017941163
ISBN: 978-1-62672-316-0

Our books may be purchased in bulk for promotional, educational, or business use.
Please contact your local bookseller or the Macmillan Corporate and Premium Sales Department
at (800) 221-7945 ext. 5442 or by e-mail at MacmillanSpecialMarkets@macmillan.com.

First edition, 2018
Book design by Dezi Sienty and Andrew Arnold
Printed in the United States of America

Drawn with a Staedtler Mars Lumograph 3H and Eagle Chemi-Sealed Turquoise Drawing pencils 3H and 4H. Inked with a Pigma Micron Size 08 and a pentel pocket brush pen. Circles made with a No. T105 Timely Circle Template, straight lines made with a Staples steel ruler and a Wescott plastic see-thru T-square. Lettered using an AMES Lettering Guide, and colored in Photoshop CS5 with a Monoprice Tablet.

1 3 5 7 9 10 8 6 4 2